Happy housing George!
All my love
                 x
              Hannah

Project editor Makkie Mulder

Art directors Janine Couperus, Elise Yüksel

Picture coordination and composition Heleen van Gent,
Mirjam Roskamp

Line extensions coordinator Mieke Beljaarts

Copy editor Merlijn Wessels

Text Chris Muyres

Practical section text Marleen Janssen,
Mirabelle Scheelings

Photography Alexander van Berge, Mirjam Bleeker, Dennis
Brandsma, Frank Brandwijk, Hotze Eisma, Paul Grootes, Luuk
Geertsen, Peter Kooijman, Anneke de Leeuw, Louis Lemaire,
Otto Polman, Jim Plasman, Jeroen van der Spek, Hans Zeegers

Styling Julia Bird, Bastiënne van Bockel, Frans Bramlage,
Fietje Bruijn, Irene de Coninck, Nans van Dam, Désirée van
Dijk, Anne Draayer, Marjan Godrie, Linda van der Ham, Kristel
de Jong, Mariëlle Kampshof, Rianne Landstra, Linda Loenen,
Marianne Luning, Bertien Minnigh, Nina Monfils, Moniek
Postma, Mirjam Roskamp, Olga Serrarens, Reini Smit, Frans
Uyterlinde, Petra de Valk

Illustrations Frans Bramlage

With thanks to Ilse Dekker, Edson Goes,
Marianne van der Lei, Addy Otto, Melina Zevenhuizen,
Marjolein Blank, Ank van den Boogert

Publisher Peter Schönhuth

Printing co-ordination Mieke Dekker

Lithography Litho Spirit, Amsterdam

Printed by Brepols, België

Published in 2002 by Conran Octopus Limited
a part of Octopus Publishing Group
2–4 Heron Quays
London E14 4JP

www.conran-octopus.co.uk

UK edition translated by Guy Shipton in
association with First Edition Translations Limited.
Jacket design by Megan Smith

First published in 2001 by VT Wonen
© Sanoma Uitgevers bv, Hoofddorp 2001

British Library Cataloguing-in-Publication Data. A catalogue
record for this book is available from the British Library.

ISBN 1 84091 259 6

INTRODUCTION BY ALI HANAN

chicMODERN

CHOOSING STYLES, COLOURS, MATERIALS AND FURNISHINGS

conran
OCTOPUS

CONTENTS

introduction by Ali Hanan

The homes of daydreams are captured on these pages. These interiors are not designer homes. They are not unattainably perfect, nor glitzy show pieces. What makes these homes so covetable has nothing to do with what's in vogue now. Instead, this book offers a portrait of modern living. It's contemporary and it's beautiful. Most of all, it's somewhere you will want to live.

'Chic Modern' is defined by four distinct styles: Simple Chic, Easy Living, Modern Rustic and New Romance. Underpinning this ensemble are timeless, elegant looks, but they are all firmly grounded in practicality. Kitchens look chic, but peer beneath the veneer and you'll see they are food workshops. Bedrooms become seductive boudoirs, but despite their allure, they're still places to sleep. Bathrooms turn into quiet sanctuaries, somewhere to rouse yourself gently before going to work or to relax at the end of the day. These homes are real homes – where real people eat, cook, relax and play. These interiors not only look good, but they work.

In Simple Chic, modern stamps its style on tradition. It's a luxurious interior cocktail, spiked with patterns like pinstripes and herringbone, but its undertones are classics, like parquet floors and high-backed chairs.

Next, there's Easy Living. Even the words 'easy living' evoke images of life with a slow rhythm. The mood is captured with generously large floor cushions, deep sofas and visually sedate colour schemes. This interior is as laid-back and relaxed as a chaise longue.

Thirdly, there's Modern Rustic. Here outdoors comes indoors. For those with a passion for nature, this embodies it. In the Modern Rustic interior, foot soles tread on warm wood; bodies scrub with sea sponges and dry off with rough-weave linen towels; food is cut on large wooden boards. Raw linen curtains mix with weathered-wood chairs and old leather armchairs sit with stone floors.

Lastly, there's New Romantic, pure interior poetry. Unlike any of the other looks, it has a beguiling charm of its own. Swathes of sumptuous fabrics allay hard edges. Intimate rooms are Byronic backdrops for a sensual lifestyle. It's a fresh, but dreamy look that allows you to indulge your most decadent tastes.

The styles are meticulously documented with visual examples and explanations. Each chapter distills the style into its essential elements. The foundation of the looks, its colours and materials are detailed along with how it works in each room.

Life isn't about daydreams. Your home, too, can look like the interiors shown here. Choose a style, personalize it and use the practical information in the second half of the book to help you realize it. The address book is designed to help you find products and services.

Pour over these pages, then take your inspiration and put it into action. Transform your own home. Pick a style. Interpret it. Give it your own twist. Whatever you do, live your own interior dreams.

CHIC

'Simple chic' is a contemporary interpretation of the classic interior.

This sophisticated mood is reflected in a love for rich materials,

timeless designs, traditional furniture and luxurious finishing touches.

Wood, wool, herringbone and pinstripe, gentle shades of grey and

elegant shapes all have a part to play. A desire for simplicity and

harmony keeps the mood contemporary and provides a delightfully

discreet platform for the presentation of traditional luxury.

SIMPLE CHIC

Dark wood with a formal, light backdrop is a striking combination for this simple but elegant house. As a consequence, the rest of the space can be filled in a far more informal fashion.

The warm glow of natural materials sets the mood – the rich patina that slowly develops on wood, veneer, leather, stone and silver. The materials employed should not only exude warmth but also feel delightful to the touch: strokably soft mohair, the undulating grain of wood, voile as thin as gossamer, unblemished porcelain. Vivacious accents are provided, for example, by the glitter of gold or crystal. Greys, whites and natural hues are the most important colours, highlighting the stylish silhouettes of the furniture. Darker types of wood such as teak, wenge and jatoba are the perfect choice because of their colonial roots and sober strength. Classic weaves such as herringbone and pinstripe are occasionally interspersed with a baroque motif or a modern geometric pattern.

luxury

Moulded ceilings, tall windows and herringbone parquet flooring form an ideal basis for this style. These details can even be incorporated in a house that does not have any original classical features. For a well-proportioned room, panelling immediately creates a stylish framework, into which the mantelpiece, doorframe and radiators can be fitted perfectly. Floors are finished with great care, and can be designed to order, such as parquet laid in alternating patterns with decorative borders following the line of the walls. The contemporary fashion is for fewer but larger decorative elements. Contrasts between light and dark wood, formal and elegant lines, and smooth and rough surfaces are accentuated in daytime by sunlight and softened at night by the warm light of standard lamps.

the basis

the entrance

The foyers of traditional townhouses are a great source of inspiration for the contemporary hallway. A simple single-colour surface with a wooden dado rail is all that is needed to create chic, elegant wainscoting. Stone looks warm when combined with wood or sisal. Choose shades of grey that are both distinguished and friendly. Laid diagonally to the walls, the traditional block pattern tiles come to life.

In the sitting room, it is crucial to achieve a balance between style and comfort. Upholster the furniture in serene tones to draw attention to its inviting qualities: the softness of the cushions, the beauty of the symmetry, the warmth of the wood. Chairs and sofas are best covered in natural materials such as wool and linen, and fabrics should have simple designs, such as a pinstripe.

sitting

The dark woodwork and elegant armchairs bring a stylish touch to this room; the contrasting colours adding a hint of liveliness to this peaceful space.

A generous chaise longue, a sober felt cube, a sofa in a sophisticated pinstripe and an original art deco design with its stately straight back. Here rustic airiness meets urban sophistication to create the ultimate simple chic interior that is fresh and individual.

sitting

eating

The dining table is somewhere you can enjoy yourself with accessories and add or reduce the level of luxury as appropriate. You may want to deck the table for a lavish and extravagant celebration or, another time, for a more formal occasion. Add extra lustre to the dinner with a crystal chandelier and a silver service, while a beautiful old table certainly adds a touch of style and of tradition to breakfast.

The dining table comes into its own in this room. The tablecloth, the chairs placed around the table and the chandelier above recreate the grandeur of an exclusive restaurant in your home.

A beautiful Vermeer-style floor is the leitmotif for the kitchen/dining room on the opposite page. The contrast of light and dark has been thoughtfully maintained to ensure a balanced space. Chinaware creates an attractive display in the glass-fronted cabinet and objects such as the books and the desk lamp challenge the typical kitchen atmosphere and turn this into a true living environment. Antique damask is always a success as table linen. For a modern, transparent accent choose a bright, white organza, as seen below left. Use your intuition to create a modern table setting with an eclectic mix of the most beautiful styles, shapes and colours. The richly imaginative dining-room chairs and crockery (below centre and right) are all different yet together display a lively unity.

eating

The lampshades and the wrought-iron fittings add a classical touch to this kitchen. The use of materials plays just as important a role – stone surface alongside blond wood and galvanized metalwork – as the spacious dimensions, the calm proportions and the superb workmanship.

cooking

This page, left: its tasteful grey tones and professional qualities make hardened aluminium into the material for the stylish kitchen. Next to this you can see crockery in timeless shades of white from milk to cream. A mixture of favourite styles and shades, old and new, will make your crockery cupboard unique and personal. While the kitchen shown opposite may look similar to that on the previous pages in terms of colours and materials, it is the distinct style of the furniture and accessories that determines the atmosphere, while in the previous kitchen the mood is created by a balanced overall design. As seen far right, a bluestone work surface with taps based on authentic originals is irresistible. Consequently, it remains a combination that is repeated in many modern kitchens.

cooking

sleeping

Every piece of furniture adds distinction to this bedroom: an unusual glass-fronted cabinet instead of an ordinary cupboard or chest of drawers; an antique wooden table instead of a dressing table. The sophisticated elements, such as the painted panelling and the charming bed, are in lively contrast to the broad, rustic planking on the floor.

In the bedroom, the classic mood is equated with sensory pleasure since this is where the skin comes into contact with fabrics and materials. Choose everything literally by feel: take the most comfortable bed linen you can imagine, a thick carpet or a soft rug for bare feet, a woven throw that immediately signals its quality visually, and materials that ensure complete relaxation and comfort in terms of colour, design and texture. This is what these pictures illustrate. What they also reveal is the timelessness and gratifying serenity of whites and greys used in the bedroom. Combine them with calming natural tones for a slightly warmer and earthier feeling. A high skirting board, as seen below right, instantly gives your walls a more elegant appearance in the simplest possible way.

sleeping

bathing

Bathing or showering in luxury and style can be one of the most enjoyable ways to relax. The look of the bathroom can easily enhance that experience, as original-style fixtures and fittings, chrome pieces, and, lastly, but not least, classic wooden furniture can be treasured in their own right. The size of the bathroom is of less importance, because much can be achieved with a well-planned layout.

A half-height partition wall separates the shower from the washstand, which itself sets the tone of this bathroom. The wall is placed at a right angle to the bath, a particularly compact solution that capitalizes on the available space.

Two bathrooms in stylish shades of grey are shown below. The niches above the bath to the right have been accentuated to create a charming illusion of panelling. The broad vertical stripes of the bottom left picture evoke chic bathing pools of yesteryear, while a wicker bench injects a little liveliness amid all the straight lines. On the opposite page, a bathroom has been given a sophisticated twist through the use of gold taps and the beautifully finished washbasin unit. On the right, radiators often determine the look of a room, which is why sought-after old models are being made again. The photograph far right is a detail from the compact bathroom on the previous page, which, despite its small size, is still able to provide the luxury of a double shower.

bathing

Working from home is becoming more popular as the use of the Internet and email increases. It is important to take this into account when designing the layout of a house. And, although it may appear contradictory, a study or working space at home can also offer tranquillity and a pleasant working environment. If well designed, it can be equally suited to reading, writing, meditating, daydreaming or listening to music.

Being able to reserve a separate room for oneself at home in order to work is something of a luxury, but a corner of the living room can serve just as well. Given that the place where one works must ideally be as comfortable yet as stimulating as possible, it makes sense to ensure that everything is to your taste, down to the smallest detail. Treat yourself to the luxury of writing with an elegant fountain pen on stylish letter paper. Beautiful things will still look attractive, and not look like clutter, even if you leave them lying around. With carefully chosen accessories and furniture, a workspace located in the living room can be a real bonus and add style to an interior.

Furthermore you no longer have to use traditional office furniture. An antique table can be employed as your desk, with solid kitchen shelving for your library. If you have devoted a lot of care and attention to creating the style of an interior, it is a shame if your working space then departs from the tone you have set. There is a rich choice of desk accessories to choose from – which, alas, is less true of the now-ubiquitous computer and printer. Their hi-tech design means that computers seldom combine well with classic furniture. A laptop is one solution if you wish to avoid the problem altogether. Another option is to hide the computer from view using a suitable piece of furniture.

The choice of chair can be as problematic as the computer. Ergonomically designed furniture is often unattractive to look at. Designer chairs, on the other hand, can provide an exciting contrast, especially modern classics such as Gispen or Eames chairs, which look good even in a subdued, sophisticated environment. Otherwise, consider using a comfortable dining- room carver chair. Whichever style you choose, you match the height of the table to the height of the chair: if necessary, it is relatively easy to raise the height of a table by adding castors to the legs. If you have a separate study then the incorporation of an easy armchair or even a sofa may be perfectly feasible for reading. Work permitting, you really will be able to sit in comfort. A classic solution!

The opposite page shows a study/library in which the desk stands free in the middle of the room. This is an agreeable option since you will not be simply staring at a wall and the desk is then accessible from both sides. The chair opposite right is not only stylish but functional: it can be spun and rolled around on its castors. This page, left: a workstation built in behind antique panelled doors that you could buy second-hand from an architectural salvage yard. If you made the cupboard a little deeper or incorporated a pull-out leaf in the work surface, a desktop computer could also be installed here. When working with a computer screen, the ideal lighting is from the side or above. Right: stimulating books and objets d'art lend the impression that inspiration is never far away.

working

storage

Peace and harmony cannot exist where there is chaos. Your eye needs to be stimulated, so pile your favourite books and magazines in a decorative fashion. This tranquil office, with its self-effacing wooden pieces and the low chest, provides ample storage space, while keeping the walls pleasantly bare. The chest is plain, but elegant, and the beautifully made cardboard boxes offer flexible storage.

EASY LIV

ING

'Easy living' calls for deep sofas, outsize cushions, carpets and chaise longues. The tempo is slow, the rhythm peaceful. The relaxed house is furnished, first and foremost, for your comfort, to make you feel good, while modern design and technology are only included if they contribute towards your domestic comfort. The underlying principle of this style is a flexible living environment with a unique identity that fully ministers to your physical and spiritual well-being.

EASY LIVING

The most important piece of furniture in this typical 'easy living' interior is its comfortable carpeting. It is a totally open living-space surface on which you can spread out a couple of cushions, and curl up next to the fireplace for complete relaxation.

Intuition is the architect of the 'easy living' house. It guarantees a completely individual result – your most personal feel-good-factor style. Colours and materials should be bright, functional and sensual. Plastics and man-made fibres are just as appropriate as wood and stone. Try aluminium next to leather, steel alongside wicker and concrete combined with felt – the unifying factor in the furnishings is comfort, a friendly character and fluid lines. Classics are combined with contemporary designs and just as easily with non-design items. The contrasts between gloss and matt, rough and smooth, hard and soft, brilliant and diffused light ensure that there is plenty of variation. Modern equipment, from a violet-coloured computer to a widescreen TV, is also an integral part of the interior.

bright

Easy living is synonymous with flexibility. The functions of spaces are not demarcated into rigid zones. Instead, living spaces overlap each other. Neighbouring zones tend to share the same colours, materials, finishing touches and furniture. The house has an open-plan character, though not at the expense of privacy. No material is too exotic or hi-tech for the floor, as long as it feels good underfoot or, at least, is practical if it is in daily use. Quality of life in your surroundings should be your barometer of taste. The walls are generally sober and virtually bare; partition walls are free-standing and movable. Display or shelving units are also used to create separate zones. Light is abundant but diffused, using matt glass and semi-transparent fabrics, for a calming effect.

the basis

the entrance

Simple, creative solutions can be found everywhere in an easy living house, starting with the hall. They are usually simple, practical ideas that are doubly useful because they are not only perfectly in keeping with the house but make it quite unique. In the photograph opposite, scaffolding-type poles have been transformed into coat hangers while also giving the hall an immediate sense of calm order.

An open-plan layout in the sitting room ensures that there is air and light as well as creating a very relaxed atmosphere. This works perfectly with roomy seating and low tables. Floor cushions, rugs and throws can fill any empty space. You can then combine a variety of materials and styles as well as move them around easily to alter the size or location of a sitting zone according to your needs.

sitting

Two chaise longues side by side in an ideal position for relaxation, while also combining the comfort of a sofa with the flexibility of separate armchairs.

sitting

A deep, spacious, L-shaped sofa with an island footstool/coffee table. These large, but low-lying pieces of furniture keep the room open and light.

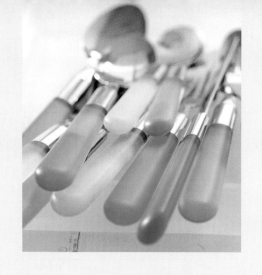

eating

The kitchen, living and dining rooms will often overlap seamlessly in an easy living home. Depending on your mood, this style allows for the flexibility of either a proper sit-down meal or just simply eating out of bowls on the sofa. The food may be quick to prepare, but it is nevertheless full of flavour and attractively presented and served – even worth laying a stylish table for, if you wanted.

It is typical of the easy living lifestyle to have furniture that blends with the environment. This adds to the airy feeling, as shown by the open crockery cabinet in this crisp, fresh dining room.

These pages clearly show how spaces overlap one another: there are no doors, the floor is continuous, a unifying colour is maintained and, finally, the furniture is not tied to one specific function. Dark linoleum gives body to the high-ceilinged space in the photograph on the left and displays the lighter tones to advantage. An attractive set of crockery is part of a relaxed lifestyle: bright in terms of colour and sheen, solid but still elegant in its form. The half-height wall, right, provides an extra dining zone, while, on the other side, slightly lower down, there is a large work surface. The fresh green of the plant and the pale yellow of the designer chairs provide accents of colour that help to soften the overall impression of cool white.

eating

cooking

Free-standing modules give you the freedom to create a layout that suits you. Here, the kitchen has been subdivided into two islands, ideal for those who love to cook socially. Even a computer fits into this contemporary kitchen.

The easy living kitchen is well equipped and its layout is practical. Below left, a sliding-door system has been employed, which, as seen here, has efficiently converted a niche into a crockery cabinet. In the centre is a designer hob, chosen by someone with a feeling for functional beauty. The same applies to the choice of tap, right, with its fluid design and softened matt finish. Opposite, left: a substantial stainless-steel work surface with professional appeal. The orange curtain helps retain a casual feel in what would otherwise be a very stark kitchen. The industrial-style units, right, have been given a friendlier look through the choice of a reddish-brown wood set against the light tone of the wooden flooring.

cooking

Everything surrounding this bed would
be equally at home in the living room: the
Starck chairs, the big cupboards, the two
low dressers at the foot of the bed, the
parquet floor. They only serve to make
the bedroom even more comfortable.

sleeping

DICHTBIJ

ik zie lichtjes in je ogen
kom eens heel dichtbij

ik zie mij

ogen zijn twee spiegeltjes
zie jij dat ook bij mij

Hans en Monique Hagen

ik noem je: bloemen
ik noem je: merel in de vroegte
ik noem je: mooi

ik noem je: narcissen in de nacht
waaroverheen de wind strijkt
naar mij toe

ik noem je: bloemen in de nacht

Jan Hanlo

The easy living bedroom is a true living space with all the luxury that goes with it, including, ideally, an en suite bathroom. In the spacious bedroom shown opposite, a free-standing wall creates a screened-off dressing area in front of the wardrobe. The floor is concrete, which provides a striking contrast with softer materials. Below left: the luxury of a room with French windows opening onto a patio. Deckchair-style stripes accentuate the sunny ambience. Centre: exploiting the flexibility offered by one space to the maximum by having a widescreen TV that can be rolled smoothly from the sofa to the bed. Finally, right: a multifunctional bed that allows you to have breakfast in bed, then replace the breakfast tray with a laptop and, in the evening, the television.

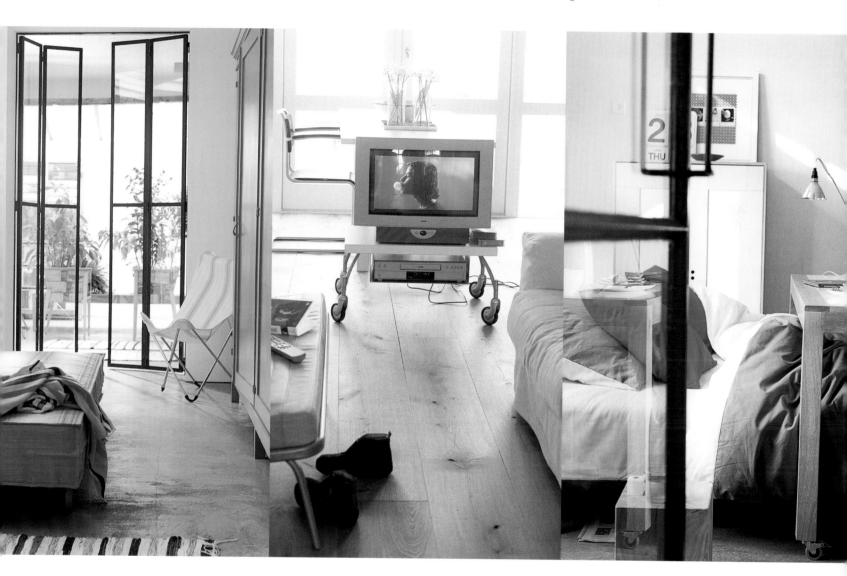

sleeping

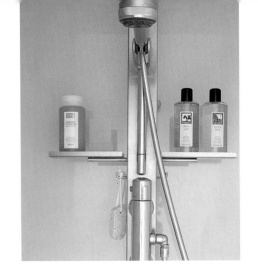

bathing

The bathroom should be a haven of tranquillity and fulfil your every desire. You will inevitably have to make a few compromises when you decorate, but try not to compromise too much on your bathroom. The ultimate bathroom will have everything you could want for your spiritual and physical well-being. In the mornings it is functional, at other times of the day it is a luxurious room where you can relax completely.

A multifaceted solution for a bathroom is a double wall in which to hide all the plumbing. If the double wall is positioned as here, you can also create new storage space. Should you site the wall further into the room, you could place a shower unit behind it. When positioned squarely against the main wall and at half the height of the room, this wall is ideal for a suspended toilet-bowl attachment with the cistern hidden inside the wall.

Here the partition wall between the bedroom and the bathroom has been removed and partially replaced by sandblasted glass. The striking red wall shines warmly through this, creating a glowing zone in which to bathe, relax and work out.

bathing

Standard solutions are rarely ideal in a room that you want to have completely tailor-made for its users. In typical layouts, the bathroom is an enclosed unit, but this is at odds with the easy living principles of flexibility and open space. In contrast, the open bathroom combined with the bedroom is a contemporary luxury that is the very essence of easy living. Sometimes, this can be achieved fairly easily by removing a dividing wall, but you should always make sure that ventilation is adequate and plentiful.

The result of this conversion is a great feeling of spaciousness. A new area is created in the house that is directed specifically towards relaxation and escaping from the pressures of daily life. A space where doing nothing is also a pastime because it revitalizes you. You decide which needs are to be addressed, be it simply resting, working out, weight training, watching TV, listening to music or reading. In short, anything that refreshes the body and spirit to give you inner peace or help you re-energize.

However, a combination bathroom—bedroom is usually not very convenient for a family if there is no additional bathroom for the children or if you plan on inviting guests to stay. There are other options, however. You could consider a multi-functional bathing area in the attic or in the basement. Otherwise, you could renovate an adjoining room that is accessible from two separate bedrooms and may even have a window. Emphasize the room's individual identity by choosing furniture and accessories that were not originally intended for the bathroom: an old wooden chair, a designer stool, a garden table, a glass cabinet, a stainless-steel hatstand, a ladder used as a towel-rail, a porcelain plate or dish for the soap, a pretty cup and saucer instead of a plastic beaker. Fashionable designs and hi-tech appliances (jacuzzi, steam bath, halogen lighting, radio) can be mixed harmoniously with old washstands, bathtubs, taps, mirrors and radiators. Fans of the hard-wearing industrial look can indulge in gleaming white tiling and stainless steel everywhere. Add stacks of luxurious cotton towels to soften the impact. You can also include a few gentler, sensual touches by using milk or matt-finish glass, a shower curtain that hangs fluidly and colourful accessories.

Plaster walls have a less stark effect than tiles. Either leave the plaster untreated or else paint it in your favourite colour. Distempering the walls with limewash is particularly suitable for damp spaces because this will hold back the growth of mould. In addition, this natural kind of paint comes in the most attractive range of fresco colours. If you have an old bath with feet, it can be made more eye-catching still by painting the exterior an attractive colour. And putting a few flowers in the bathroom can really bring the room to life.

working

Your workplace should also have a relaxed mood to match the
rest of your home and to keep you feeling fresh and inspired
while you are working. Take this room, for example, with its
soft carpeting in a warm, natural tint. This adds warmth and
complements the aluminium and plastic furniture, while the
large swivelling rollers give the table a useful mobility.

The study does not really exist, in the strict sense of the word, in a flexible living environment if only because working is merely one of the things for which a computer is used. Surfing the Internet, artistic creativity, playing games and communication are also important functions. In the morning, breakfast can be eaten at the table below left, while you catch up on your emails. At other times, the table becomes a hard-working surface, with room to spread out papers. On the opposite page, left: you can peek behind the free-standing partition wall. On the other side is the bed and on this side fitness equipment, a computer table for two and Arne Jacobsen's classic 'Egg' chair to snuggle up in. On its right is a multifunctional table with all the connections for equipment within reach.

working

storage

The photograph on the left shows the space created behind a free-standing partition wall at the top of a bed. This has created a walk-in or, rather, a walk-through, wardrobe as well as a dressing area. The wardrobe is closed off by glass and fabric. To the right is an open wardrobe. Using two open cabinets linked by a plank above, a space is created for a rail, treating the clothes as stylish display objects.

MODERN

'Modern rustic' is a style that seeks a connection with the outdoors by employing natural materials, subdued colours and discreet decoration, as well as by making good use of the garden or patio in the home. It is a style whose sole aim is to create a familiar environment – consider, for example, Shaker style and Scandinavian simplicity. The ultimate goal is an interior that naturally resonates both contemporary elegance and modern-day tranquillity.

MODERN RUSTIC

The trees can be moved
outside, depending on the
season, as you can see from
the weather-beaten pots, and
the comfortable floor cushion
is perfectly placed to catch
all the available sunshine.

The raw materials for the 'modern rustic' interior come from nature: wood, stone, leather and wool, as well as zinc, wicker and twine. As these materials age, they develop a much-valued patina that lends their appearance character and life. As a rule, materials that are essentially 'strong' are allowed to reveal a gentler side, giving a solid foundation to the contemporary feel. Thus wood is aged, limewashed or soaped, developing a new surface without detracting from the material's depths. Natural tones are mostly used, together with natural colours that have a modern character, such as olive green, sea blue and sunny orange. An emphasis on living nature is also brought into the home through the deployment of larger plants and even small trees.

pure

Wood and stone are the materials typically used for flooring in the modern rustic interior, as well as sisal, wool and marbled linoleum, while rugs and fleeces are also suited to this style. Walls are plastered, painted, whitewashed or distempered. Outdoor areas are incorporated in the design as far as possible – a conservatory allows you to live on the border between outdoors and in. Windows are kept as free of ornament as possible to let light through unimpeded, whether in abundance, diffused or in rays of light, while a single design object can accentuate the whole mood. Keep in mind the parameters of the design: it is much easier to incorporate the more sturdy, robust and heavy elements of modern rustic in a farmhouse than in a brand-new housing development.

the basis

the entrance

The hall is the pivotal unit between the outdoors and indoors. To make the transition seamless, choose materials and finishing touches for the hall that are also used outside. Opposite, the young trees in olive planters enhance the rustic effect generated by the materials used in this hallway. The door shown above exhibits the simple beauty of an old traditional stable door made from pale oak.

Seating is all about pure ease and comfort. In this style, the furniture is all about soft shapes and plump cushions. Its frame or construction can sometimes be left on display, to highlight its intrinsic decorative value. Modern design is also at ease in the 'modern rustic' house, especially if it is expressing simplicity or else a powerful feeling of its creation from a single piece of raw material.

sitting

The coast can inspire a house with outdoor tranquillity just as much as the countryside. This interior shows the unmistakable influence of the beach house with its wall planking, weathered floorboards, blue tones and open French windows.

sitting

With three sets of French windows opening onto the outdoors, the full expanse of the garden can be brought into the living room. Add to this the broad, sturdy floorboards and comfortable sofa and you now have the basic elements that make this sitting room so comfortable.

eating

The day can achieve a natural, relaxed rhythm of its own if you allow time and space to enjoy meals. Mealtimes are, above all, occasions to gather and talk, and the informal, warm atmosphere of the country dining table is ideal for this. Everything on it and around it is pure and honest, from the furniture to the crockery and, more often than not, robust earthenware that is easy to use and feels good to the touch.

A contemporary interpretation of a centuries-old solution: the central hearth or stove. Here, the stove is at eye level, creating a window between the kitchen and the dining room. The walls have been limewashed, a natural covering with a silky sheen. The weathered wooden furniture and the elegant Thonet chairs complete the mood.

The two large tables on these pages play a central role in these living spaces. They are used for everything: from reading the newspaper to working and spending the evening entertaining guests. The collection of wooden chairs around the table on the left both personalizes the room and enlivens it. To the right is a modern designer table that, nonetheless, fits perfectly into the character of the dining room because of the solid simplicity of the design. The wood has been limewashed so the table and bench do not appear too heavy or clumsy. This table is used for eating from one side only while the other side is for reading or working. Basic accessories form part of this style, even in as 'primitive' a form as the breadboard depicted in the centre.

eating

The rustic feel is reflected in the rough floor tiles and the tap – a strikingly elementary design. Amid this is a great deal of stainless steel – from a luxury espresso machine to a designer stool and a professional chef's trolley – the modern element in this kitchen. What binds these elements together is their unembellished and durable quality.

cooking

Cookery is different in the country. Much more importance is attached to fresh ingredients that have a rich flavour and good quality. Fast food is also far less prevalent. In that sense, modern rustic may be more than an interiors style but rather a lifestyle in which the kitchen forms the basis for the good life.

The table plays a key role in such kitchens. Moreover, it is not only aesthetically desirable to choose a large kitchen table that is sturdy, but practical as well. Within the rustic style, food is often prepared on a kitchen table, especially if cooking forms a part of the social life.

When thinking of a country kitchen, what comes to mind is a large space furnished with diverse elements, old and new mixed together: work benches, racks, cupboards, a large cooking range. In this kitchen style, the crockery and pots will be on display for their commonplace beauty, with pans suspended above the work surface. This is also often the most practical arrangement, as seen in a professional kitchen. Everything is within easy reach and you never have to search in the backs of deep cupboards. Fresh vegetables, fruit and herbs are always a refreshing sight and are not usually hidden away either. Plus, they also contribute towards the seasonal mood.

In a smaller open kitchen, racks and individual items may look too crowded and messy, in which case a better option is perhaps a built-in kitchen, especially if you want to deal with the space available as efficiently as possible. You could dispense with cupboards above the work surface because this gives a more spacious feel and often has a less severe effect. The art of what to leave out characterizes a style whose premise is simplicity. For example, time and energy is saved if you choose simple kitchen utensils and equipment. Machines have to be set up time and again and keeping them clean is even more costly in terms of time. Experienced cooks know that you are often better off working with a good set of kitchen knives than with a whole host of kitchen appliances.

There are two types of things that are continually mixed in the rustic kitchen: articles that are full of life and character and items of simple quality that function without any fuss. From a technical point of view, the stove is the most basic tool in the kitchen. For this type of kitchen, you should choose something stylish, from a real Aga to a smaller model with visual references to the past in its copper detailing and decorative finish. Even a stainless-steel unit will not be out of place because the difference between modern design and nostalgia is nowhere as relative as in kitchen appliances. American refrigerators with their streamlined designs that were once seen as futuristic are now seen as reassuring, slightly rotund friends from the past.

It is a great luxury to have a lot of space to work in kitchens, especially if several people are cooking at the same time. If you do have a large kitchen, the most important piece of furniture will be a central kitchen table. The semi-open kitchen below right can be closed with large 'stable doors'. However decoratively and seductively you may display your kitchen accessories and foodstuffs, it is sometimes desirable to be able to screen off the kitchen from sight. Opposite left we see bowls in a huge variety of natural colours, from jade green to jasmine blue, beautifully contrasted with the wood tones in the rustic kitchen. Opposite right is an open kitchen whose country character derives in particular from its large oak work surfaces and the warm, earthy use of colour.

cooking

sleeping

Comfort and cosiness are the two most important qualities for your bed. Luxury is appreciated best when set against an unpretentious backdrop. You can achieve this effect by, for example, only giving the walls a rough finish. This style also works very well if the furniture around the bed has a slightly improvised look about it, such as a wooden block or old chair serving as your bedside table.

The walls of this room have been painted grey using a paint that has a granular texture. The carpet, although soft and comfortable, has a similar look. The reclaimed planking for the headboard completes this room's air of restraint.

The bedroom opposite has a pleasingly peaceful aura because the floor, the partition wall and the door have all been painted in gentle shades of grey. The vitality of the wood is soothed a little, though the cosy, warm feeling has certainly not been lost beneath the paint. Turning to bed linen, the rustic bedroom benefits from the use of luxurious cotton or linen in unassuming, natural colours. The employment of wood and stone paving could hardly be more solid or bolder than in the photograph below centre. Nonetheless, they have a gentler side here: the modern rustic style in its purest form. To the right is a robust variant on the theme of romantic four-poster beds: full attention has been devoted to the practical comfort of the bed linen.

sleeping

bathing

The atmosphere of your bathroom can have a significant effect on the whole bathing experience. For one person, luxury can mean gold taps, while for another it is a far simpler approach. In the modern rustic bathroom, there is little to detract from the water and the soap. The room will not only appear more welcoming from the use of a lot of wood but will also have a warmer resonance to it.

The custom-made wooden surround of beech plywood makes this bath so remarkable that the room does not need anything else. The pure minimalism employed here has an extremely natural character.

Two relatively small bathrooms yet with a spacious feel to them. The white bathroom, left, is completely timeless but also state-of-the-art thanks to the neutral colours and the simplicity of the design and materials. Since it is all so robust and basic, it fits perfectly in a self-assured style like 'modern rustic'. The basis of the other bathroom is also quite restrained, which immediately makes the room look pure and natural. All the woodwork has been painted in a shade of grey to which a drop of red has been added for warmth, while the large window establishes a strong link with the outdoors. Decoration is barely present – only in simplicity of form of the functional objects, such as towel-rails, taps and blocks of soap.

bathing

Below you can see nature in the form of office accessories: pencils made from twigs and a diary and notebook with hefty leather covers, while various items seen in the studio to the right have been chosen because they create an ambience and are extremely functional as well. The tough locker gives the firm impression that it can take a few knocks and an old kitchen table has been used for a work surface, so a few marks here and there will not matter. Tables of this kind often contain a drawer, which can also be useful. The stool on castors and the ceiling lamp act as a couple of modern accents. The overall impression created is of a deep serenity since, despite all the robust materials used, everything has been given a lot of light and space.

working

Paving bricks give this studio area, opposite, a real workshop appearance and also break up the surface of the floor. Old shop cabinets create a lively partition wall filled with countless small drawers. The cabinets also act as a dividing wall between the work and living space. Below left: a working area featuring a beautiful table with a stone work surface and a solid supporting wooden frame. Centre: thick shelves faced in teak veneer have been mounted on the wall in a way that disguises their support brackets, which means that the desk merges in very subtly. The American filing cabinet to the right is typical of the unique piece of furniture that can establish a workroom's character on its own.

working

storage

On the left is an original scullery sink and the cupboard. Authentic pieces like this are of vital importance to create the right ambience in a house so try to retain them and wherever possible, renovate only the cupboard interiors. To the right is a functional storage system composed of cabinet units. The handmade bowls and the shell collection are testament to the owner's love of nature.

NEW ROM

Bright floral colours, sumptuous flowery prints and real flowers betray

the return of the romantic. The romantic look is fresher and purer than

ever, replete with adventurous choices and esoteric combinations. The

designs are decorative but soothing, the lines may be baroque but are

crystal clear, the ambience is dreamy but never sentimental. An

experience for all of the senses: the colours startle, the light sparkles,

the scents are of springtime and the textures are richly varied.

NEW ROMANCE

Ornamental wallpaper, stimulating colours, curved wrought iron, exotic flowers,
a classical pillar and a baroque chair – anchored by a warm carpet in a neutral
natural colour. 'New romance' in its purest form.

One of the most appealing aspects of new romanticism is that it allows the house to sparkle with colour. These much sought-after shades are best described as the gentle pink of roses and the blue of cornflowers and they immediately bring a house to life. Furniture is a mixture of styles, native and exotic, old and new, re-upholstered for originality and a longer life. Objects, such as lamps, are sometimes given an individual decoration of their own – much depends on the emotional value you attach to an item. Fabrics are best selected on the basis of comfort, embroidery because it looks so sumptuous, accessories because they fire the imagination, accents of gold to achieve a kind of fairy-tale glamour and flowers because they bring a life of their own to a house.

colour

A city loft apartment, a renovated warehouse, a farmhouse, a brand-new home – a romantic interior can be created in almost any building. Use wood for flooring if you long for the natural look, whether plain, painted or gilded, or carpet if your taste is for softness underfoot. Wallpaper with floral, striped and toile de Jouy motifs imparts a warm, familiar atmosphere to a room, while glowing paint colours allow the walls to speak. Light streaming through windows should be gently filtered by the thinnest voiles and choose lined curtains made from shiny fabrics. The refreshing element in new romanticism is the deliberate contrast between design and the baroque. A contemporary new romantic environment is a space whose frivolous features always stand out.

the basis

the entrance

'New romance' is a warm and vivacious style that always beckons you into a home. Allow the hall to show only an alluring foretaste of the atmosphere created in the rest of your house. A small, sparkly chandelier, for example, or simply a taste of the colours and lines to come. Decorative ironwork is particularly appropriate and this will make a small entrance feel quite spacious and imposing.

The living room is filled with elegant furniture in a variety of styles. Sinuous wrought iron, elegantly carved wood and brightly coloured glass can all be combined to great effect. Baroque furniture can also be effective if its dramatic style is toned down a little by a slightly more restrained material. Conversely, plain furniture can be covered in fabrics with exuberant and colourful designs.

sitting

This chaise longue may be rather formal, but is also exceedingly comfortable, a quality that can be lacking in the more romantic styles. Here it is the embodiment of new romanticism, simply by being covered in a strikingly exuberant floral fabric. The small still-life arrangement next to the plain wooden doors is a subtle romantic touch.

sitting

A parquet floor and light, plain furniture form the basis for a bright interior in which there is nothing superfluous or lacking. The cheerful pink used for accessories creates striking accents and the iron gates create a unique decorative partition.

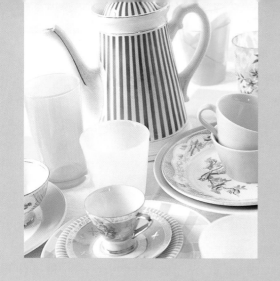

eating

A romantic dinner should be set in exquisite surroundings, but they should nevertheless be relaxed. The most important consideration is enjoyment – ideally of all the senses – in the food, flowers, cutlery, table linen and with soft music playing gently in the background. However, you can also find romance in simpler, everyday things, such as breakfasting at the kitchen table using the best silver.

This minimalist table with its fairy-tale glamour is utterly individual: the coloured glassware, the silver tablecloth and, in particular, the translucent organza with pockets for displaying small decorative objects.

An amalgamation of styles often produces the greatest surprises, such as the combination of French sophistication and the vibrancy of the exotic shown opposite. Just as eye-catching are the lampshades decorated in trendy stripes above the tastefully chosen dinner service and the vase filled with classic romantic flowers, such as roses and carnations (below left). The table next to this has been laid with an instinctive feeling for colour and form. Ornamental flowers have been placed in green and red water: a simple idea that creates an immediately festive impact. On the right we see a 'rustic' interpretation of this look with elegant white-painted woodwork and crockery set against a background of fresh green, patterned wallpaper.

eating

cooking

The ingredients for the kitchen are chosen either for their visual effect or else for their function. Pure emotional choices are juxtaposed with the purely rational. Thus stainless steel is at home next to well-worn wood and a stark work surface can be placed against a shocking pink backdrop. All this conspires to make the kitchen a stimulating, fun place in which to work, eat and be together.

A shocking pink wall and a shiny red floor set
this kitchen alight. Colour determines everything
here, while form is subordinate since simplicity
characterizes the 1950s chairs, the bare light
bulbs and the stainless-steel cooker.

The back of the teak dressers has been removed to reveal the blue wall tiles behind to give the cabinets and their contents a cheerful freshness. Right: the cupboard doors have the romantic simplicity of a farmhouse kitchen but also a futuristic gleam from the white paintwork, the zinc above the worktop and the grey concrete floor. Beauty and functionality become one in the fluid design of the stainless-steel stove, opposite page, left. A painted wall lends an orange glow to the steel. Far right: the recessed edging of the metro tiles and the rounded corners of the cupboard doors give this kitchen its charm. The mahogany used for the worktop and the floor generates warmth, while the lavender blue of the cupboards adds a romantic touch.

cooking

The bedroom is the place for dreaming. It is the heart of a house for the romantically inclined. The ultimate example of the romantic bedroom is one that is pure white. The absence of colour allows an unimpeded perspective on the essentials of texture, pure materials, embroidered or beaded fabrics – an amalgamation of subtle touches that might not normally be noticed. Naturally, this kind of immaculate whiteness is impractical and inevitably becomes sullied. Yet even that ageing is a part of the romantic spirit – like that special feeling generated by things that can last only a short time, such as the smell of newly ironed linen or that freshness after a rainstorm.

Candles and flowers are the simplest way to enhance the romantic feeling in a house. Another contributing factor is a certain nonchalance about your surroundings. Let it appear that everything just happens to be where it is, quite by chance. You can achieve this in the bedroom by having lavish bed linen that is somewhat loosely thrown, even crumpled, on the bed, by adding throws, blankets, quilts and rugs that can be moved around or taken away. This creates a relaxed mood that remains vital and fresh. Because the romantic feeling is so personal, an intense colour in the bedroom can work just as well as pure white. To maintain the tranquillity of the room, it is usually a good idea to restrict yourself to one basic colour but to employ different shades of it throughout. Patterns such as stripes and flowers will soon generate the right atmosphere if used in moderation. In most cases, the piece of furniture that determines the overall image has to be the bed. A four-poster or canopied bed is far and away the very definition of romance, though simply a bed with a mosquito net draped above it can make an attractive alternative. Antique, wooden-framed or wrought-iron beds are other possibilities. However, you can just as easily use a normal bed and envelop it in a profusion of draped bedspreads and bed linens. Install a dramatic headboard – even the suggestion of one will suffice. Make it from old wood panelling, an attractive frame or simply paint one on the wall. In a modern home, living-space functions often overlap each other or are combined as this makes the house more flexible and gives it a greater unity. It is usually most convenient to integrate into the bedroom, other relaxing areas such as a bathroom. The bathroom benefits because it will acquire more space, while the bedroom at once becomes more luxurious. In the modern romantic bedroom, you can also incorporate features that create a true living space where, apart from sleeping, you can also relax, read, listen to music, eat breakfast or watch a film. A real bonus to this style is to have a bedroom adjoining a balcony, patio or garden to bask in the sunshine: try to achieve this if at all possible.

The bed hides beneath the duvet. The duvet cover, in turn, has been covered with a polka-dot voile that lends a slightly magical appearance to it. The patterns are restrained but provide vivacity against the deep reds and dark wood.

M 23 Oct

A romantic mood can be created easily in a house without old features. This has been achieved effortlessly in the (literally) poetic room opposite, even with surprisingly ascetic furniture. The four-poster takes much of the credit, of course, as well as the perfect subtle choice of colour for the soft carpeting. Below left: an antique quilt, striped rugs and a pink coverlet create a mood of informal comfort. The two designer lamps add to the tone of the room. One captures the frivolous feel, while the other expresses elegance. Right: the wonderfully uncomplicated mirror standing on the side table and the striped wallpaper, which appears so nonchalantly painted, exemplify the relaxed simplicity so characteristic of new romanticism.

sleeping

bathing

Romanticism in the bathroom can be created in many different ways. An old galvanized-iron bathtub or a bath with feet both have qualities of their own that can easily compete with the latest trends in jacuzzis and steam baths. A warm, seductive ambience is equally important as the fittings. Comfort can be particularly emphasized through extravagantly thick bath towels and the use of luxurious materials.

A concrete floor is the epitome of austerity, yet the beauty of the bamboo and the antique bath spring to life when set against it.

Tiling is notably absent in the bathrooms shown on these pages. A clinical glaze of enamel is not essential to keep surfaces clean and polished. Good paint or plasterwork serves just as well. If you find chrome too stark, the warmer shine of nickel-plated taps may be the solution, as shown opposite. The designer radiator is an unexpected choice but fits in astonishingly well with the overall style because of its restrained elegance. A bathroom's personality is created through unique finds, such as the mirror, below left, with its etched-flower frame. Centre: Far Eastern simplicity was the premise for this bathroom, turning bathing into a ritual. The charming, round shower curtain to the right could easily have come from a French hotel: a romantic alternative to the standard shower cubicle.

bathing

Whatever the kind of work to be done, the working environment in the 'new romance' interior is stimulating and pleasurable, informal and full of emotion. Even the accessories, such as the colourful sari-covered books, are pretty rather than businesslike. Right: an old kitchen table serves as a desk in the middle of the room – home and work do not have to be grimly separated from one another. These tables often contain a drawer, which makes them particularly practical pieces of furniture. Opposite: technology does have its blessings. The laptop, for instance, makes it possible to work anywhere, wherever you happen to feel like working at the time, be it in the garden or the bedroom. Nowadays, thank goodness, you can also work on a laptop that looks great too!

working

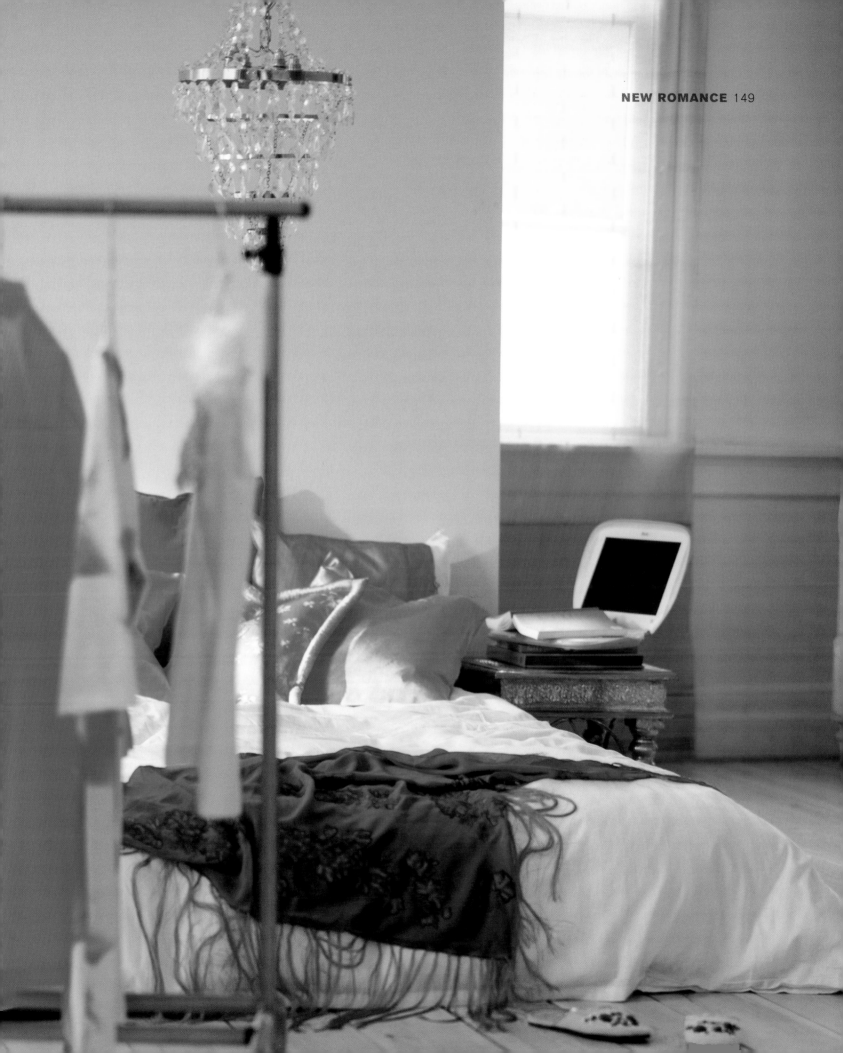

storage

On the left, a large linen cupboard has been made from old panelled doors. A few items have been left on display: the patterned cushions and the pink dress inject immediate colour and exuberance. Similarly, the wrought-iron chair with its decorative curves also lightens the overall image. On the right are shelves of functional objects, creating a simple, but attractive display that requires no further adornment.

PRACTICAL

Perhaps the only problem with flooring is the fact that there is simply so much choice: wood, carpet, linoleum and stone are just a few of the options. In addition, underfloor heating is available for just about all floor types, making them particularly pleasant to walk on barefoot.

WOOD

A wooden floor is still the most popular choice. There is dark or light and hard— or softwood. Pine is a softwood, while oak and jatoba belong to the hardwoods, which are more expensive. The hardness of wood is indicated by a number: the higher the number, the harder the wood and the more resistant it is to damage. All wooden floors perform their function, however, no matter how hard the floor is. Depending on how the floor has been laid (either separately from the subfloor or glued to it), it may expand or shrink under damp, cold or warm conditions. Also, a wooden floor can discolour from direct sunlight: light-coloured wood will darken, while darker wood will fade.

Parquet

This is a collective name for a number of types of wood flooring. Parquet can involve planks of wood but also comes in the form of battens, or blocks, which are laid according to a pattern. Carpet parquet, for example, is made of solid parquet blocks. A well-known form is the herringbone pattern. A thick false floor of chipboard is first glued or nailed to the subfloor to provide a base for the parquet to be laid on. The parquet blocks are then glued and nailed in place on the floor, piece by piece. The nail holes are filled and afterwards the floor is sanded, polished and, finally, protected with oil, wax or varnish. Laying this type of floor is a job for a professional. Also available is solid mosaic parquet that has been pre-glued to a base of paper or webbing, which holds the patterns together. This makes laying the parquet much easier and it can be done without professional assistance. This type of parquet can be

glued straight onto a concrete subfloor. A false floor will have to be placed on top of the subfloor, if the latter is wooden, in order to create a level surface. The surface can be finished once the parquet is in place. The parquet floor cannot be taken up again and moved. Before refurbishing an old parquet floor, first check its thickness. A sanding machine can be used if the floor has a solid-wood top layer at least 4 mm (¼ in) thick. However, a floor that is only a couple of millimetres thick is best handled by a professional, either with a sanding machine or by hand.

Wood laminate and veneer parquet

Wood laminate parquet – a layer of parquet a few millimetres thick on wooden boards with tongue and groove – is relatively quick and easy to lay down. Polishing and varnishing is not usually necessary because wood laminate parquet is usually provided with a hard layer of varnish in the factory.

Wood laminate parquet is laid as a floating floor (but can sometimes be glued). The subfloor (chipboard) must be level enough to allow this. Wood laminate parquet can also be obtained in an oiled finish and several bordered designs can be bought with which to lay an ornamental floor. A cheaper alternative is veneer parquet, which looks like wood laminate parquet. This floor has a varnished parquet layer of 0.6 mm and can be laid using a click system.

Wooden floorboards

Carpet, mosaic and laminate parquet all create a smooth surface. A floor that is made of floorboards appears livelier and more robust. Floorboards come in various thicknesses and widths. Softwoods are usually cheaper and the fewer knots a piece contains the more expensive it becomes. Floorboards can be laid on a wooden floor as well as a concrete one. An additional subfloor is sometimes required: this levels out the surface, providing soundproofing, water resistance and even weight distribution. If the floorboards are laid without an extra floor, you should at the very least incorporate a damp- and soundproofing layer. The empty space between the subfloor and the upper floor can seriously exaggerate sound. Soundproofing material can be bought on a roll: it insulates the space and contributes to a mere 3 mm (⅛ in) increase in floor height. Once the subfloor is ready, the floorboards can be laid and then sanded. Then they are varnished, given a coating of oil or waxed. A combination of oil and wax also exists – hard wax, see below – and some floorboards have already undergone treatment with this in the factory.

Varnish/lacquer

Varnish is always applied to wood in several coats. You can walk on the floor two days after the final application of varnish. A varnished floor will always shine a little: damage is therefore more rapidly visible. White scratches in the varnish sometimes occur but repair kits can be bought to eliminate these small blemishes. Note: clear varnish is often slightly yellowish. Coloured varnishes can be obtained to transform, for example, your pine floor with a walnut look. Of course, you can also colour your wooden floor with wood stain or varnish. This can be done using a colour varnish, a clear varnish mixed with a wood stain or a top-coat paint. In anticipation of wear and tear, you should decide on a tough paint or a special kind of floor varnish. 'Ordinary' paints and varnishes can be used too, provided that a durable, clear floor varnish is applied over them when dry.

Wax

A floor that is to be waxed must first be impregnated to fill the pores in the wood. This makes the floor more resistant to penetration by dirt and spillages. The floor can be waxed after this treatment, further protecting it and giving it a natural appearance.

Oil

Oil penetrates deeply into the pores of the wood, just like an impregnating agent, and comes in a variety of colours. The floor can be whitened or, conversely, darkened. After sanding, the floor is usually treated with a base oil to which pigments have been added. Afterwards, this oil-treated wood is specially soaped for protection. A floor that has been coloured with an oil treatment must be well maintained using a special maintenance oil that eliminates any worn spots, scratches or blemishes. Details of treatment and upkeep will be available from the supplier.

Hard wax

Hard wax is a combination of wax and oil, and comes in a variety of colours. It can be applied directly to sanded wood and acts as a protective layer but it does have to be carefully maintained.

Synthetic laminate

Laminates can also mimic wood. The top layer is composed of a 'wood photograph' with a strong layer of varnish applied on top. In addition to wood effects, laminates can also be obtained in sisal, stone or even metallic designs, with a tactile quality. Metallic laminate has a thin top layer of high-grade steel. For a decorative design, laminated floorboards can also be interspaced with insert pieces in a tile format. You could also combine various differently coloured laminates from one supplier, or laminates that come in a variety of patterns. For example, you could have an oak-coloured laminate floor in a herringbone pattern edged with a mahogany-coloured border.

A laminate floor can be laid as a floating floor. Some retailers incorporate a useful click system: this makes the floor easy to lay and just as easy to remove when moving house. Laminate can be laid on nearly any smooth surface, though a damp- and soundproofing layer does need to be laid underneath. Repair kits can be bought in the appropriate wood colour for touching up any small blemishes.

Cork

A cork floor is composed of grains of crushed tree bark that are heated and compressed into tiles or wide strips. A cork floor is usually made up of several base layers with a very thin veneer of cork on the surface that determines its design. A wear-resistant layer of lacquer is applied on this. Cork is strong, warm to the touch, a good soundproofing agent and reasonably priced. Because of cork's elasticity, it is not easily damaged. Indentations from furniture usually restore themselves easily. Cork can be glued or laid as a floating floor with a tongue and groove system. A special kind of cork flooring has a top layer of wood veneer. A soundproofing layer of cork is placed between two layers of wood. This parquet flooring is laid as a false floor and is suitable for rooms above the ground floor. The wide-strip parquet format makes it easy to install.

TIP

If you want to varnish a floor another colour, you no longer have to apply the coloured varnish first followed by a protective coat of lacquer. If you use a polyurethane lacquer, you can apply colour and protection in one coat, saving time.

CARPETING

Carpeting makes a room feel warmer. In addition, it insulates and soundproofs the floor. It is possible to lay carpet in patterns or strips to create an utterly unique floor. If you want to delineate separate areas visually in a room, especially in an open-plan layout, you could lay one colour of carpet for, say, the office area, and another for the living zone.

Carpet must be laid on a completely level surface. Floorboards alone are not adequate as the gaps between the boards will soon become visible through the carpet. Hardboard or chipboard should be put down on the floorboards first before laying the carpet. The type of backing of the carpet then determines the way it should be laid. Carpet with a foam backing can be glued straight onto the floor beneath. Underlay is generally recommended for carpet with a textile or rubberized backing.

Various kinds of carpet

The visible part of the carpet is called the 'pile' and can be made of wool, hair, cotton and other natural materials or from artificial fibres, such as polyamide (nylon), polyacrylic (acrylic), polyester or polypropylene. There are also carpets made from sisal (agave fibre), coir (coconut fibre), sea grass and paper; all of these are organic fibres and come in all kinds of formats. The colours are however restricted to natural tones (from cream to brown) and black. There are also sisal stair carpets. Carpet backing may be made from (a mixture of) jute, cotton, flax, hemp, foam rubber, latex or synthetic materials. The appearance of the pile is determined by the length of the threads and whether the threads have been cut or not. Bouclé carpeting is made of looped threads that have not been cut, to create a bulkier effect.

STONE

Stone is cold to the touch, but that can be countered by installing underfloor heating. The colour, shine and structure of a tile determine the effect it will have on its surroundings. Terracotta tiles (reddish-brown, matt, uneven) come across as much warmer than white, shiny floor tiles. Yellow Moroccan concrete tiles also give out more warmth than a grey concrete floor.

Ceramic tiles

Ceramic tiles are usually made from clay and water. The clay is baked, so hardening the tile. Ceramic tiles will usually have been glazed; if not, the tiles may be porous and will have to be impregnated before use so that they will be able to withstand soiling or spillages. Ceramic tiles come in many shapes and sizes, including ceramic mosaic tiles.

Natural stone

Natural stone is the collective expression for various kinds of slate, granite and limestone. Every tile, flagstone or load will be slightly different. Therefore, when ordering, take into account that your consignment may differ regarding colour and structure from the example that you have seen in the shop. Natural stone can be employed in a variety of ways. When a flag or tile has been smoothed it means that, while smooth, its surface will not be gleaming. A polished tile does shine. The tile may also have been barrel-polished: in this process, tiles are 'washed' in a centrifuge with small porcelain chips which slowly abrade the tiles. Barrel-polished tiles have an attractively aged appearance. If the tile has been cut, its sides will be less sharp and straight than if it has been sawn. In natural stone, therefore, a great deal of attractive variation is possible. In addition, slate and quartzite have a natural propensity for splitting, which means that their surfaces may be uneven.

The format of tiles can vary markedly as well. So you can obtain marble in strips 30 cm (12 in) wide in free lengths (i.e. various lengths in one batch), there are tiles of 40x40 cm (15x15 in), 50x50 cm (20x20 in), and also mosaic tiles measuring 1x1 cm (½ x ½ in). Tiles and mosaic tiles can be combined but do take note of their difference in thickness.

The thickness of natural stone tiles and flags varies from 1 to 2.5 cm (½ to 1 in). A sturdy, level base is important when laying a natural stone floor. It is not a good idea to try to lay this type of floor yourself.

The glue or cement must be allowed to harden once the floor has been laid. Afterwards, any cement residue must be removed using a non-acidic product to avoid any damage. The floor must always be impregnated since natural stone is porous.

CAST OR POURED FLOORS

A cast floor is made on site. Cast floors have a smooth appearance because they contain no joins or seams. It is also possible with some cast floors to have a base

TIP

A wooden floor needs a dry base to rest on. A lot of moisture often still remains in a newly built home, so wait at least eight weeks before laying the floor to allow the subfloor to have dried out. Plastering also adds a great deal of moisture to a house, so wait six to eight weeks after this job before you start to lay the wooden floor.

board included in the casting. In the bathroom, the floor can be cast with a gradient so that the floor declines towards the drain for the shower. Cast floors must only be installed by professionals.

Concrete

Concrete is being used more and more in our homes. It has an industrial appearance because of its grey colour. A concrete floor has a uniform look to it but is never completely smooth: fine hairline cracks appear over the course of time. In fact, these irregularities are what give character to the floor. When a floor has been poured (in a 3 mm/⅛ in) layer) it is then polished and lacquered for protection, which gives it a slight shine. You can wax the floor if it has to be largely watertight, with wax that ranges from matt and high-gloss to transparent. Floor maintenance depends on the finish it has been given. You can also colour concrete with pigments, stain or concrete dyes. A professional will know which substance is most appropriate for the desired result. Synthetic flooring is available as an alternative if you want only the appearance of a concrete floor.

Terrazzo

Terrazzo is a mixture of cement with pigment and small pieces of marble, glass or mother-of-pearl that can be obtained in a wide variety of colours and designs. Your floor level will be raised by an average 7 of cm (3 in) after pouring the terrazzo mixture. It does, however, require a stable and robust subfloor, such as cement. Floorboards would have to be removed first and then you would have to see whether the joists and ties were strong enough to support such a floor. Afterwards, dovetailed zinc plates are laid on the joists to distribute the weight of the concrete equally. A layer of concrete is then poured onto the plates, followed by the terrazzo mixture. Other materials can also be included with the terrazzo, such as mosaic tiles or glass and even lighting!

Polyurethane

Polyurethane poured floors are more elastic and warmer to the touch than concrete or terrazzo. They come in all manner of colours: even granite-type styles are available. A rubberized mat of 5 mm (¼ in) thickness can be laid beneath the poured floor for soundproofing. The base does not need to be uniformly level, though, if it consists of floorboards or tiles, some levelling is advised in order to avoid visible joins. The thickness of the poured floor will be between 2 and 7 mm (⅛ and ⅓ in), depending on its base. The floor is finished off with a matt coating. It will have a lifespan of 20 to 30 years.

Gravel flooring

A gravel floor is composed of millions of river gravel or quartz granules that have been combined in an epoxy resin to form a flooring material.

There are many colours available and there is often a slight sparkle to this flooring. It is also possible to pour patterns, so you can create a border to contrast with the centre of the floor. Decorative gravel can be laid in any room, though sometimes a different subfloor will be necessary. Once the floor has been poured it is then finished with a water-resistant, shiny top layer. Constructing a gravel floor is a job for a professional.

Linoleum

Linoleum, made from natural, raw materials like linseed oil and resin, is a smooth and hygienic floor covering. It can be used throughout the whole house, except in the bathroom (due to the room's high level of humidity). This kind of flooring can be obtained in many designs, bought by the roll (2 m/6½ ft wide) or in tile form. There is also adhesive-backed linoleum sold on strips of MDF (medium-density fibreboard) measuring 24x120 cm (10x48 in). This can be laid on any floor base (wood and concrete); small patches of unevenness are levelled out by the MDF. The subfloor does have to be level if you choose linoleum from a roll because you will have to glue the linoleum to the floor base. A professional should lay linoleum from a roll.

Vinyl

Vinyl is principally composed of PVC. In recent years, however, vinyl has improved markedly in quality. A new development is vinyl with a wood print where the knots can be actually felt and the shine looks realistic. There are also selections of ornamental and tiled designs, for example in a combination of matt and gloss finishes. Vinyl can be obtained in 2 m (6½ ft) and 4 m (13 ft) widths, as tiles and in strips in the approximate format of wood laminate parquet. The floor must be smooth when laying a vinyl floor. It is glued to the floor base in large rooms but can be laid unglued in rooms with a floor surface area of less than 40 m² (430 ft²). There is a very special kind of woven vinyl that has a real textile structure. It can be obtained in a variety of colours and (striped) designs. Woven vinyl is watertight and can also be laid in the bathroom or on a balcony. It is a flexible material and is not cold underfoot.

Rubber

The practical aspects of a rubber floor are that it is water-resistant, fire-resistant, non-slip, soundproof, antistatic and extremely wear-resistant. Rubber looks a little like vinyl but has a slightly rougher surface. It can be laid anywhere in the home without the need for a professional. Rubber is available in many colours and designs and is sold on the roll (width 120 cm/4 ft) and in tile form. Rubber is glued to a smooth floor base.

Several materials in one floor?

It is often aesthetically appealing and practical to combine several materials together in one space. For example, below the worktop in the kitchen lay a broad band of tiles meeting the wood floor in the rest of the room. A flooring specialist will have attractive solutions for these transitional zones, such as special profiles for the flooring components. Do take account of any differences in height and the effect on the wood.

Underfloor heating

Theoretically, heating can be laid below all types of floor, though it may suit one floor better than another. It is not possible under foam-backed carpets, and jute-backed carpets require electric underfloor heating.. 'Soft' flooring is less suitable as it does not conduct heat as well, so it would be inadvisable to employ it as your sole means of heating. Stone floors conduct heat best. The effect on the heat should be taken into account in the case of a wooden floor. The plumbing must be evenly distributed under the floor and the water temperature may not rise above 40°C (104°F). A parquet specialist will be able to tell you which wood types are most suited to underfloor heating.

walls

Wallpaper, paint and plaster are the traditional, and still eminently suitable, materials for decorating our walls. Alongside the familiar designs and colours are clever trompe l'oeil effects and modern colours and textures. But there is now also a much wider choice of wall coverings: what about loam plastering or firmly fixed wooden panels? These techniques create exciting effects that can turn an ordinary space into something quite special and distinctive.

Wallpaper

A good-looking result is quickly achieved with wallpaper. Not only will it over slight flaws in the wall, but it can also help to disguise a room's proportions. Many wallpaper collections also feature plain or complementary borders with which to create horizontal as well as vertical linear effects. Wallpaper is also available with dado designs for areas such as the hall. There is an overwhelming range of colours, designs and textures from which to choose. Always ask for a sample before buying, so you can hang it in the room and see how it looks.

Wallpapers differ in quality. Some types (especially the vinyl varieties) can be wiped clean and – if of sufficient quality – can be used in the bathroom as well. At the back of wallpaper books you will see various symbols indicating how the wallpaper has been manufactured and in which rooms it can be used.

Dry-strippable wallpaper is in the ascendant at the moment. This wallpaper is much easier to put up than the traditional kinds. You apply the paste only to the wall and, if the wallpaper needs to be removed, it can be simply pulled off the wall, without any need to use a steamer. Dry-strippable wallpaper can be translucent so do make sure to use it only on light backgrounds. There are also wall coverings with finishes in cotton, wool, linen, viscose, jute and silk. They are rather costly but do have a long lifespan and need only vacuum cleaning every now and then to maintain their beauty.

In general, wallpaper must be applied to a smooth surface. You can apply new wallpaper on top of old wallpaper if it is still firmly attached. If the wall is uneven, you will need to hang lining paper first. The removal of old layers of wallpaper is best done using a wallpaper steamer (which can be hired from DIY stores) and a filling knife. You can use a liquid filler to deal with any holes made in the wall, which means you can be slightly less careful when removing the paper.

Plastering

Plastering a wall involves applying a layer of plaster of Paris to the wall that afterwards can be given other finishes if so desired, for example incorporating a series of sweeping arcs or running a plasterer's comb through wet plaster to create a ridged effect. The wall can also be given a smooth finish. The surface on which a wall is to be plastered must be properly water-resistant. For that reason, a base of wood or softboard is not suitable as a surface. Special plasterboard can be obtained for plasterwork. Transitional zones where different surfaces meet (a concrete wall that forms a corner with, for example, a plasterboard wall) must be 'bandaged' with a kind of gauze webbing that works as a bridge between the differing properties of each material. This will prevent unsightly cracks from appearing later on. Sometimes, a wall has to be primed to ensure a proper bond.

Plastering will create a great deal of dust and moisture in a house. It may take quite some time before all of the moisture is gone from the walls. Plasterwork is easily painted over and is suitable for bathrooms (unless ventilation is inadequate). You could also just leave the plaster unpainted to create a lovely, rustic look. Ready-coloured plaster is also available.

A wall smoother product can be used to apply a smooth layer of plaster. Smooth plasterwork can be made wipe-clean by applying an acrylic coating to it. Before coating the plaster, you could give it a wash of colour or paint on patterns, stripes or letters. There are also products on the market to help you create relief work in plaster, such as curves. Colouring the wall in an appropriate shade can strengthen the Mediterranean effect still further.

Loam plastering

Loam plastering is a special kind of plasterwork. It comes in a variety of natural colours that can be mixed together, while pigments can also be added to it. The colour of the loam depends on the minerals in it. Iron, for example, will turn it terracotta red. Loam plaster can be applied to an undercoat of loam or to primer on plasterboard, concrete or other walls. Loam plasterwork is not suitable for areas that are liable to get really wet, such as shower units, although it can be employed behind a washbasin, for example, as long as it has been impregnated beforehand.

After application, loam plasterwork dries to leave a sandy surface. After drying, it can be brushed to prevent it from shedding dust. Several manufacturers supply loam plaster and you will find it in shops selling environmentally friendly products.

Paintwork

Paint is a very cheap and simple way to change the look of your walls. Several kinds of emulsion paint can be bought for walls – matt paint, paint that is easy to paint over and water-soluble paint. These paints are available in a satin look. In addition to countless standard colours, you can select a shade from the colour chart and have it specially mixed. Compare colour charts and consider using a tester pot of paint first because the colour you choose may look different at home from the way you imagined. Virtually any colour is possible: there are even emulsion paints in silver and gold! Try to buy all your paint at one as the colour can vary very slightly from batch to batch.

Some kinds of emulsion are environmentally friendly; some are suitable for use both indoors and outdoors. You can paint walls using flat-edged brushes or a roller, using narrower brushes for edges and details. There are many different kinds of roller on sale, including non-splatter rollers, special rollers for applying designs and rollers with a coarser nap specifically made for walls with a relief. Tape off the

TIP
Leather is the latest and most luxurious material for covering walls and floors. Leather-look wallpapers are also available as a cheaper alternative.

window and door frames and so on beforehand, using masking tape designed for the purpose. If you are planning to paint lines or stripes, or if you are going to paint only a section of a wall, choose a type of masking tape that is less likely to leave marks behind.

Effects using emulsion

Ceilings can be made to look higher by painting a strip of wall 25 cm (10 in) deep just below the ceiling in the same colour as the ceiling, preferably white. Stripes on the wall also influence a room: horizontal stripes or lines will make the room appear wider; conversely, vertical stripes will make it appear higher.

If you tape off the wall at a height of 1.25 m (4 ft), painting the lower section a different (preferably darker) colour than that above will create a dado effect. You could also decide to separate the two colours with a 3 cm (1¼ in) band of contrasting colour. Applying patterns or letters in silver paint onto a colour background is an attractive option and best achieved with the help of a projector that casts the image onto the wall, allowing you to trace over it. Tracing with carbon paper is also effective.

Limewash (distempering)

Limewash is a matt paint to which natural pigments have been added, and it is suitable for indoor and outdoor use. Limewash is a very old method of decorating walls and, consequently, is also suitable for historic buildings.

Wood

A completely different effect can be generated if you attach wood to a wall in the form of panelling or wainscoting, an effect that was very popular in the past. Panelling can be custom-made for you by a carpenter or can be bought from the building trade in do-it-yourself packs. Of course, you can also experiment with wood: builders' merchants and timber yards sell blockboards in various sizes and various wood and veneer types.

Paint and stain for wood

Paint or wood stain can be used to protect wood. Wood stain breathes (and regulates moisture content), while paint is good as a sealant. Paint for wood comes in a gloss or satin finish and there are also variants that are environmentally friendly, acrylic (water-based) and turpentine-based. Water-based paint dries faster than turpentine-based. You should remember that an acrylic paint does not adhere well to a turpentine-based paint and vice versa. Wood must be well sanded before it can be painted. Remaining coats of paint must be removed completely, which is best achieved using a paint

scraper in combination with a hot-air stripper. You can also strip paint using chemical agents, although these are very harmful to the environment and the area in which they are being used must be well ventilated. After chemical stripping, the surface must be neutralized with water and a little ammonia and once this is dry you can start to paint.

Tiles

Tiles are incredibly resilient, easy to keep clean and are often used in areas that are prone to wetting — in the bathroom or around the kitchen work surface. However, tiles can also be used for decorative effect. As well as ceramic and natural stone tiles, there are also glass tiles (in a variety of shapes and sizes), stainless-steel tiles, glazed and unglazed finishes, handmade or antique tiles. These are often expensive but can always be used sparingly as accents or borders in a plain tiled wall. Tiles can vary greatly in colour, so try and buy your tiles in one go. Grout attracts dirt and mould easily, but stain-resistant grout is now available and it also comes in a range of colours to match your tiles. Cutting tiles to go around corners and sockets can require some skill.

TIPS

Buy a strip of steel (3–5 cm/1½–2 in wide) from a hardware store and screw this horizontally to the wall at eye level. You can then attach favourite photographs and drawings to this by using magnets. A steel plate could be used instead if you want to create a large display area.

A vinyl wallpaper 2/3 mm (⅛ in) thick has been produced specially for wet areas. It has to be hung using a special paste, but its surface is washable, stain-resistant, impact-resistant and scratchproof.

You should always remove masking tape immediately after painting, otherwise some of the new paintwork can be pulled away with the tape if it has had a chance to dry. The longer masking tape is left, the more difficult it is to remove. There are now special kinds of tape that you can leave for longer or that are specially suited to particular surfaces.

Painting a wall in a child's bedroom or in the kitchen with blackboard paint is eye-catching and useful, especially if your child has a short attention span. In the past, this paint was only available in black but it now comes in all kinds of colours. You could also paint stripes or blocks, of course, for a more dramatic effect.

As well as a floor surface, concrete can also be used for walls to create a smooth, industrial-style and highly innovative effect. A variety of colours is available.

the bathroom

Practical planning and layout are important if you are building or renovating a bathroom. Increasingly, though, creating a comfortable space hinges on well-designed fixtures and sympathetic decoration, whether a bathroom is being enjoyed for a long soak in the tub or just a quick shower.

Draw up your wish list

If you want to build, change or renovate your bathroom, first start by drawing up a wish list. The most important question is what you want to do with your new bathroom. Will there be one washbasin or two? Do the washing machine and dryer have to be found a space as well? Are you installing a lavatory or a bidet? Have you decided on a bath and separate shower or a combination of the two? All these things have to be itemized before the work commences. As well as meaning you can start looking for the right fixtures straightaway, this will also clarify whether your plumbing and electrics will need to be extended.

Next, you should consider the layout. A bathrooms specialist can help you with this but you can also do it yourself using squared paper. Remember to leave enough space for movement and turning around. For example, a space of 70 cm (28 in) in front of a washbasin is the minimum for somebody to pass behind you comfortably. If the bathroom has a pitched roof, as in an attic conversion, you must not forget that this will mean less 'effective' space. A lavatory, for instance, requires adequate standing room.

To create a clear picture of your ideas for the bathroom, it is useful to make a collage of the materials, colours and accessories that appeal to you.

The bath

The base measurements are important when deciding on the size of the bath. (Note: if someone refers to a bath of 180x80 cm (71x32 in), this always means the outer measurements, which may differ from the base dimensions.) A large bath is not per se the most comfortable: a smaller person will not get any support for their feet in a larger bath, something that is far from relaxing. Wherever possible, you should test out a bath in the shop by lying in it. If you like to share a bath, choose one with adequate room, a plug in the centre of the tub and an inclined backrest at both ends. Measurements aside, there is an enormous variety of bath designs, interior and exterior. There are baths with rectangular exteriors that fit well next to a shower cubicle, but many are rounded. Models that are free-standing can be fitted with a surround or else placed on feet. Free-standing baths give you more leeway when deciding where to deploy them in the space available. To find a bath with feet try architectural salvage dealers as well as retailers.

If the bath is to be tiled in, it is practical to have the base board (at a height of 10 cm/4 in) set back slightly. This will make it easier to wash young children in the bath or when cleaning the bath itself.

Bath materials

The material from which the bath is made is as important as its shape and dimensions. There can be a big difference in price depending on the material used: as a rule of thumb, the thicker the material (i.e. the more durable), the more expensive it is. Cheaper baths are often made from enamelled sheet steel. They are easy to keep clean but can be slippery and cold to the touch. Nonetheless, steel is a good conductor and so heats up quickly. A steel bath does act rather like a soundboard when water is running into it though. Surrounding the bathtub with insulating material before it is tiled in largely solves this problem.

Apart from steel models, there are also plastic (acrylic) baths. They are more expensive but do have a lot of advantages. Acrylic can be moulded to any desired shape, plus, an acrylic bathtub feels warmer because it adapts to room temperature immediately and water will cool less quickly as a result. Acrylic bathtubs do not have pores, which means that dirty bath rings are not left behind, making the bathtub easier to keep clean. An acrylic bath also deadens the sound of the water as it fills the tub, in contrast to the relative cacophony created by a steel one. Check how colourfast the material is before buying.

The shower

A shower can be taken standing either in a shower tray or simply on the floor. Shower trays can be obtained in enamelled steel or in plastic, just as for baths. You can also get special shower trays made of zinc or stainless steel that are sunk into the floor.

You can choose between an open, walk-in shower or a sealed shower unit. A walk-in shower has side panels (tiled or glass panels or else walls made of glass building bricks) but no door. A sealed shower unit is a shower cabinet with a door. If you decide on the latter, do pay particular attention to the profiles into which the door fits. They often contain a number of ridges requiring a lot of maintenance.

There are also cubicles with steam showers: jets spurting water and steam. These cubicles are often fitted with a bench.

The glass door to the shower cubicle must always be made from safety glass. Some manufacturers treat the glass with an anti-scale product that makes cleaning much easier; there are even products you can use for treating glass yourself.

The washbasin

The washbasin in a bathroom no longer has to stand on a plinth or be attached to a wall. In the last few years, basins and bowls have increasingly appeared mounted beneath or on top of a surface. There are a huge variety of washbasin styles to choose from: square, rectangular, round, oval, wooden, stainless-steel, glass, ceramic and natural stone. A surface can be moulded from plastics like Corian to include a washbasin to create a seamless unit. These fixtures are easy to keep clean, are available in many colours and can even have the appearance of granite or terrazzo. Instead of two washbasins, you could go for an extra-wide model; wide basins like these are often constructed within a wooden or iron framework. Relatively new on the market are washbowls made of natural stone fitted into a steel frame.

The height of a washbasin is a key factor. It will depend on your body height, though, on average, washbasins are placed at a height of 85–90 cm (34–36 in). You can always put a plinth underneath an old column-mounted washbasin that is a little too low but you want to keep. This will, however, probably require some adjustment to the plumbing.

Taps

The internal mechanism and the design of taps determine their price. Ceramic discs in the mechanics will raise the price, for example, but will also guarantee a regular flow because of their resistance to limescale. Mixer taps with water quantity and temperature regulated by one hand are easy to operate, while thermostatic taps ensure a constant water temperature. When choosing the taps and the showerhead, you also need to look at how much water is needed to obtain a good flow or jet of water. The force of the flow, or the quantity of water per minute, depends on the hot-water heating (combination immersion heater, water heater or boiler) and on the diameter of the pipes. A large showerhead with a diameter of 30 cm (12 in) needs to have a good 16 litres (3½ gallons) of water per minute; when mixed with cold water, the pressure will need to be even greater to give you the perfect jet. The same applies to a shower with side-jets. To get sufficient water pressure, you may have to enlarge the hot-water heating system and install pipes of a greater gauge from the boiler.

If you wish to have a tap emerging straight from a wall, do take into account that the mechanism concealed within will require a depth of roughly 8 cm (3 in). This space must either be available within the wall or else created by building a false wall, which has the added advantage that you can hide any plumbing inside it or create additional storage space.

When choosing a new tap, note also the depth of the washbasin. A tap that disgorges from too high up will create splattering in a flat-bottomed basin. A traditional washbasin tap (intended for washing hands) that disgorges water at a low height will be difficult for drinking from or rinsing out shampoo.

TIPS

Instead of positioning fixtures against the bathroom walls, another idea is to place a free-standing wall in the middle of the room. Plumbing can be incorporated within such a (half-height) partition wall to accommodate fixtures on either side: a washbasin on one side, for example, and a shower on the other.

If you want to have the washing machine and dryer in the bathroom but would rather they were kept out of sight, why not screen them off with a frosted glass door, which can be custom-made.

Central heating

Bathroom temperature is crucial to comfort. An average temperature of 24°C (75°F) is optimal. Both electric (a mat with electric heating filaments) and traditional floor heating can be employed in the bathroom. The latter kind is composed of heating pipes laid beneath tiles and connected to the central heating system. You cannot use the floor heating independently of the rest of the system with this design, however.

The entire bathroom can be heated if you choose a type of floor heating with sufficient capacity, but if the floor heating is purely auxiliary, you will have to include a radiator somewhere else in the room.

Many tubular radiators can be used for hanging and drying towels; these can also be installed as partitions in a room. You can also find radiators that incorporate mirrors and shelves for handy, additional storage space, and bench radiators on the top of which a board is mounted for sitting on. There are also now many options with regard to colour. Some manufacturers can mix any colour and will spray-paint radiators for you in the colour of your choice. If you are choosing a chrome model, remember that a chrome radiator emits heat less efficiently than a white one.

The floor and the walls

Walls and floors in bathrooms must be watertight. If plasterboard walls have been built, perhaps to create a partition wall, then these must be green plasterboard (which is suitable for wet areas). If you have chosen wooden walls, use water-resistant glued multiply (or similar), which can be tiled. You must ensure that the base is made watertight both before and during tiling. Although tiles are very easy to keep clean, not everything in the bathroom needs to be tiled. Plaster can be used but not where it could come into contact with water. Plasterwork can be covered with an emulsion paint especially for bathrooms, which is damp-proof and gives mould less of a chance to take hold. Do not plaster the walls completely smooth because it will prevent them from breathing.

If you are putting alcoves in a wall (useful for storing shower items and towels) check that they have the same dimensions and try as far as possible to line them up properly.

Is there natural stone flagging on the floor? In that case, remember that it requires more maintenance than ceramic tiles. Natural stone will not tolerate acids or alkalis and, as a result, must be impregnated. You must not clean it with bleach or anti-limescale products, which will slowly eat through the stone: it is best to use a pH-neutral soap.

Tiles or terrazzo

The size of the bathroom may to some extent determine the size of the tiles: a small tile makes the room look smaller and more cramped, while a larger tile projects a spacious and somewhat more luxurious effect. The disadvantage of large tiles is that more of them will probably have to be cut during tiling. The sealant does not have to be white or grey: coloured sealant is available in all sorts of shades. Natural stone is fixed with a thin sealant. You can tile over the old wall if the old tiles are still level and firmly fixed.

It is not a good idea to choose shiny tiles for bathroom floors because of the danger of slipping. You can buy special anti-slip tiles with a slight relief to reduce the risk. Some tile ranges include curved skirting tiles that seal corners as well as make cleaning simpler. Tiles smaller than 20 cm (8 in) are recommended for a shower if used as flooring instead of a shower tray: this aids flow into the drainage well (with an incline). It is best to use a light grey sealant (which is less easily discoloured) on the floor rather than a white one.

Terrazzo is particularly suitable for bathroom floors, seamlessly incorporating height variations, inclines and plinths. It can be obtained in many colours and can be combined with tiles.

Wood

It is possible to have a wooden bathroom floor but it remains vulnerable to the warping effects of water. The hardest types of wood will fare the best — softwood is best avoided. All joins must be well sealed and the wood must be impregnated. Regular treatment using beeswax is also recommended as this will enable the wood to remain water-repellent. A wooden floor can also be made water-repellent by giving it at least three coats of heavy-duty varnish. One special effect is to sink teak strips into the floor, for example in front of the washbasin, creating a kind of wooden bathmat. If you want to have a wooden floor in the bathroom and you have chosen a free-standing bathtub, it is perhaps a good idea to place a slab of natural stone beneath the bath. You should still ensure that this slab has been well impregnated and that the join between the stone and the wood is properly sealed so no water can seep underneath the stone.

Mirrors

You can either attach a mirror to tiles or else tile around it. If the mirror is being positioned on a plastered wall, you can give the mirror some 'depth' by sticking it to a 3 cm (1¼ in) thick board and then hanging it. Make sure that no water gets into contact with mirrors sunk in the wall or surrounded by tiles because this will lead to black blemishes on the mirror. Make a splash border (tiled or plastered) above a washbasin and do not tile a mirror into a shower wall. A mirror above the washbasin can also incorporate extra storage space: various designs are available for use as cabinets. Mirrors can be heated with a flat mat stuck behind the mirror; this can be connected to the light switch, preventing the mirror from misting over when the bathroom is filled with steam.

Ventilation

Bathrooms must be well ventilated to prevent the growth of mould. If there are no windows, install a decent ventilator. You should take the volume of the bathroom into account when choosing a suitable ventilator: length x width x height. It is recommended that air should be replaced in the bathroom between 10 and 15 times per hour.

A ventilator can be connected to the light switch so that it starts up when the light goes on to conserve energy, although there are now also motion-sensitive devices. The majority of ventilators can be programmed to continue working for a number of minutes after being 'switched off'. A hygrostatic ventilator has a sensor that measures the degree of humidity in the air and switches itself on when the air becomes too moisture-laden.

TIPS

Not only must you take into account the location of electrics in the bathroom and their proximity to water, but you must also ensure that all permanent items made from metals are properly earthed. This also applies to items such as the pipes, the radiators and, if appropriate, the bathtub and the shower tray.

There are three kinds of jacuzzi: the first one works with air, the second type with continually recirculated water (this requires more maintenance because dirt and bacteria can be retained in the internal workings of the pump) and the last with a combination of the two. Try to find a showroom that will demonstrate models so you can see how they work and choose the one that suits you best.

Some manufacturers supply special products for treating bathroom fittings to prevent limescale from taking hold thus preventing long hours scrubbing them.

Do you want to enlarge your bathroom, perhaps to install a bath or just to make it a little more comfortable? Have a good look to see if it is possible to move part of the wall back slightly. At least 70 cm (28in) of additional width is needed to fit a bath in comfortably. An unused airing cupboard, for example, can sometimes supply you with the space you need.

The space below a washbasin can be used to good advantage for the storage of towels, laundry or cosmetics. In small bathrooms, however, it is sometimes better not to put a storage unit here. Keeping this space free creates a roomier effect and you can buy open shelving units instead.

Separate shower panels are available that are simple to mount onto a shower wall. A shower with sides can be constructed like this without the need for serious building work. Sometimes a shower-sauna system can be assembled, too, although you will need to seal the shower cubicle.

Electrics in the bathroom

You must take care with all electrics in the bathroom: water and electricity do not mix. Consequently, a bathroom should be divided into four zones. Zone 0 is wherever water is present: the bath, the shower and the washstand. Zone 1 is the area above this, while zone 2 is the 60 cm (2 ft) surrounding that and Zone 3 is the remainder. Light bulbs may only be housed in Zones 2 and 3, although not in Zone 2 if they can be reached by hand from Zones 0 or 1. Electrical switches go in Zone 3 but if possible should be placed outside the bathroom. If you want a television in the bathroom, it will need to be placed behind glass so no water can get to it. A radio can be concealed in a cabinet where no water can intrude and you can also buy battery-operated, splash-proof radios. Washing machines and dryers may only be sited in Zone 3. They must also have their own group electrical connection in the meter cupboard. Always check the regulations for the use of electrical equipment and appliances in areas of high humidity.

Splatter-proof sockets (with flip-shut flaps) may be used in Zone 2. Never place an appliance in the bathroom on an extension lead that is supplied with electricity from another room. Pull switches are generally the safest mechanisms to use.

Today, not only do we cook in the kitchen, we also live in it. That is why, alongside its functionality, its ambience is becoming ever more important. This is reflected in the enormous choice of materials for work surfaces, units and sinks.

Cooking and eating

The way in which the space is to be used determines how a kitchen looks. It is sensible to set out what you want first before a layout is finalized and the equipment purchased. The following questions may help you with this:

• Do you want to be able to join in the conversation in the room while cooking? If so, an open-plan kitchen is the solution.

• Do you want to be able to eat in the kitchen?

• Do you often cook for a large number of people or do you prepare quick meals and use the microwave a lot? In the last instance you will need a refrigerator with a large freezer compartment. Conversely, the worktop need not be so large and a four-hob hotplate will suffice. Someone who cooks a great deal is probably better off with a wider, multi-hob hotplate combined with an extra-wide extraction hood. A double sink, lots of storage space and extra electrical sockets would also be useful.

Once you have decided how the kitchen should look and you have chosen the equipment, get quotations from a number of kitchen specialists. The kitchen can also be custom-made instead of being composed of standard units.

The layout

It is important when drawing up the layout for a kitchen to create a logical order for the kitchen appliances, giving them equal amounts of space and distance from each other while still leaving enough room to work in. It is useful if the refrigerator is near the cooker and the the sink. You will need worktops 60 cm (2 ft) wide either side of a hotplate or stove. Ideally you should also have a work surface that is 120 cm (4 ft) wide, which you can create by having a pull-out or foldaway table. It is also useful to have kitchen utensils stored close to appliances. Make sure that drawers are not placed in corners, which would block the opening of other drawers or cupboards. Consider the direction the kitchen door opens; this goes for the refrigerator, too, since most models can have doors opening either left or right.

Kitchen trends

A modular kitchen does not have any long, straight work surfaces into and under which appliances are incorporated. Instead it is composed of separate modules or units for equipment, workspace and storage. These are often mounted on feet, not only practical for cleaning but also creating a roomier feel. The very apogee of flexibility in a kitchen is a cooking table that includes a stove, sinks and other equipment and fittings, often positioned in the centre of the kitchen as an island. The advantage of an island is that it is easy to walk around, so both practical and social too. Increasingly, wall-mounted cupboard units are being left out of the equation to make the room appear larger. As an alternative, you could use shelves, trolleys or a special kitchen dresser.

WORK SURFACES

A work surface must be comfortable to work on. Its height and depth are the major determinants. The average height of a work surface is 90 cm (36 in).

TIP

You can get worktops that combine wood with stainless steel. The top of the work surface, for example, might be made from brushed stainless steel but it is edged in beech multiply.

However, 95 or 100 cm (37 or 39 in) is possible, too. What, then, is the ideal working height? Hold your forearms out in front of you at right angles to your body. The palms of your hands should now be 15 cm (6 in) above the work surface. Kitchens can be specially made for very tall people with higher floor cupboards and there are also kitchen units that can be adjusted in height. Although a high work surface is useful, it is easier and safer to manoeuvre pots and pans if the stove is slightly lower. The depth of a standard work surface is 60 cm (2 ft): the deeper it is, the more space you have for storing kitchen utensils and small appliances and the tidier it will look. The material from which a work surface is made is as important as its dimensions. Is the surface heatproof, easy to clean and stain-resistant? Does it incorporate a water baffle? Can it be delivered in various colours and designs? There is a huge variety of options to choose from, to match your kitchen decor.

Wood

A solid wood worktop is composed of glued components to prevent warping. Nevertheless, wood will always react to water to some slight degree, which can give rise to the appearance of tiny splits. The surface colour may also fade in direct sunlight. Various kinds of wood are available for work surfaces. Varnish gives a wooden surface a glossy appearance; oil gives it a more natural look. A coat of varnish or oil will make a wooden work surface damp-proof but not watertight. Therefore, you should always mop up spillages as quickly as possible and do not leave wet cloths on the surface. Wooden surfaces that have been varnished or oiled may be cleaned using a mild cleaning agent, but do not use bleach, methylated spirit or abrasives. An oiled surface must be treated regularly in order to maintain its water- and stain-resistant attributes. Untreated wooden surfaces will require regular sanding. While wood does have a high heat-tolerance level, it is better not to place hot pans directly onto a wood surface.

Decorative sheet material

Sheets of MDF (or similar), chipboard or multiply are available with glued plastic surfaces that come in designs ranging from wood and stone to the purely ornamental. These sheets are smooth and non-porous, are waterproof and will tolerate a great many cleaning agents. Caustic substances, however, such as unblocking agents like hydrochloric acid, can attack the surface. Though relatively scratchproof and generally resistant against wear and tear, the surface cannot be repaired once damaged. Placing hot pans on it may cause the adhesive to melt.

Terrazzo

Terrazzo is a mixture of coloured cement, pieces of natural stone and glass.
It is poured into custom-made moulds, can include a water baffle if required and you can even incorporate a terrazzo sink into your worktop. It takes approximately a week to harden.

Cesarstone

Cesarstone is a man-made type of stone that is 95 per cent quartz and, as a result, is harder than granite. Moreover, it is scratch- and shockproof, damp- and heat-resistant, and non-porous. It is available in many colours, is easy to maintain and looks natural. It can also include a water baffle.

Granite and marble

Granite is a natural stone. The sheet material is polished to close its surface, although it may still remain slightly porous, which can cause blemishes to appear over the course of time. Granite is usually polished to a glossy finish but may develop more of a matt look through usage. It is heat-tolerant and can also be supplied with water baffles. Marble can be used in work surfaces, too, although it is expensive. However, because marble is more porous than granite, blemishes will appear more quickly. These can be removed fairly effectively with a mild abrasive. You can also buy protective marble polish.

Belgian bluestone

Belgian bluestone is a hard type of natural stone that varies in colour from light blue-grey to nearly black. It is largely composed of limestone and is sensitive to acidity. Remember that lemon juice and vinegar can mark the stone and cause damage. Bluestone can be polished or smoothed. Polishing will give the stone a shine, whereas smoothing will give it a satin sheen. Since bluestone is porous, it must be treated with an impregnating oil a few times each year to protect it from the effects of water and other substances. The stone variety known as Nero Profondo looks just like Belgian bluestone but is acid-resistant and is as scratchproof as granite.

Lava stone

Lava stone is a form of solidified lava. A glaze and colour coating are applied to the surface of sawn sheets of lava and these are oven-baked at a temperature of 1000°C (1832°F). The baking process produces a craquelé effect. Sheets of lava stone have a maximum length of 260 cm (8½ ft). Lava stone is extremely hard, scratch-resistant and hygienic because it does not have any pores. It is also heat-resistant to 1000°C (1832°F) so it is quite safe to leave a hot pan standing on a lava stone surface. Lava stone can be supplied in any colour you wish.

Stainless steel

Stainless steel has a very modern, industrial look. It is non-porous and therefore hygienic, though highly susceptible to fingerprints and scratches. The work surface may swell slightly if a hot pan is placed on it, causing a popping noise. Do not use abrasive cleaners: there are special cleaning agents for stainless steel on the market.

Ocriet

Ocriet is a mixture of granite and quartz granules melded together in resin and fibreglass. This material is non-porous, scratch- and shockproof and also becomes impermeable to staining once treated with a special stone wax.

Plastic

Several manufacturers make work surfaces from plastics. The advantage of a plastic surface is that acids and chemicals will not affect it. It is also scratchproof and easy to maintain. The sole disadvantage is that it cannot cope with heat. Plastic surfaces are moulded and a sink or water baffle can be seamlessly incorporated into the worktop. Damage can be repaired.

Concrete

One of the latest trends is to have a concrete work surface. This is cast on site and can include a water baffle if required. It will take a couple of days to harden and needs a further two weeks for curing. Concrete can be protected from blemishes by treating it with oil. It is normal to see small air bubbles (from pouring) and hairline cracks in concrete: this is precisely the material's charm.

The facing wall

The wall behind the stove and next to the taps suffers more than anywhere else in the kitchen. Therefore, it is a good idea to provide these zones with a hard-wearing material that is easy to wipe clean. All of the materials used to make work surfaces can also be used to cover the facing wall. This wall can also be tiled or painted and given a washable coating of acrylic.

The sink

There are a lot to choose from both in size and shape as well as in materials (ceramic, plastic, stainless steel, natural stone). Once again, you must ask how the kitchen is going to be used. If you have a dishwasher, for example, you will need to devote less space to a sink. There are single or double sinks: the double version often includes a draining board and/or an integrated chopping board. There are also 'one-and-a-half' sinks and 'one-and-a-quarter' sinks composed of a sink plus a small one next to it, often with a sinkhole drainer. There are hexagonal or octagonal sinks and also kidney-shaped models specially made for corners.

Taps

Kitchen taps must be accessible and easy to use. Thermostatic taps are useful because they help prevent scalding by very hot water. In practice, the water used in a kitchen is usually between 30° and 45°C (86° and 113°F). There are also taps with built-in sensors that switch them on when your hands are detected beneath them. The latest taps have a touch-operated panel with which you can programme the power of the flow and the temperature. People who like the professional or industrial look can have a tap with a pre-rinse facility, as often seen in restaurants. If the sink is next to the stove then a tap with an extendible (up to 50 cm/20 in) sprinkler head can easily reach a pan on the hotplate. And how about boiling water straight from the tap for a quick cup of tea? There's a tap that will do this for you. You can also install a water filter. When installing a tap, ensure that the water jet reaches far enough towards the front of the sink. If the tap is too far back, it often causes splattering over the work surface.

Cooking systems

It is not possible to cook with gas everywhere and not everyone enjoys cooking with electricity. Each cooking system makes its own demands on the cookware you

TIP

If you plan to have two worktops in the kitchen that will be facing each other, ensure that there is a minimum space of 120 cm (4 ft) between them. This enables people to pass by and makes opening cupboard doors problem-free as well.

use and the way you cook. People who like a smooth, wipe-clean hotplate will choose an induction hotplate, ceramic hob or gas under glass. In induction, heat is generated from the friction between electromagnetic fields and directed specifically to the base of the pan. The temperature of the hotplate itself does not rise above 70°C (158°F). Induction reacts faster to temperature adjustments you make than a ceramic hob would. Consequently, induction cooking most closely resembles cooking with gas. Electric coils mounted below the hotplate generate the heat for a ceramic hotplate. The glass heats up first before the pan does. Ceramic and induction hobs use electricity. You will always need two extra electrical groups for induction cooking and this is sometimes the case for ceramic hob cooking too.

It is also now possible to combine several cooking systems in one work surface (cooking with gas and electricity, for example) for added versatility. Several manufacturers have small, domino hob (usually dual-hob) modules that are incorporated alongside each other. Other options can include a grill plate, deep-fat fryer, wok or barbecue griddle.

Other appliances

It is wise to be as broadly acquainted as possible with the wide-ranging choice in kitchen appliances and equipment in order to make the right decision. As well as budget, you should consider whether you really need the appliance or whether it will just take up work surface. Decide how much labour it will save you and how often you will use it. Major manufacturers operate telephone/Internet information centres.

One of the latest and most useful of innovations is the built-in coffee maker and an espresso machine that can be attached to the wall, which will free up your work surface. There are dishwashers measuring only 45 cm (18 in) across that take only a small amount. Dishwashers designed for use when standing mean you no longer need to bend down when filling and emptying. An oven with a pyrolysis function simplifies oven cleaning and reduces work. The oven temperature is raised to 500°C (932°F), which carbonizes any remains. Fish and vegetables can be quickly prepared in a steam oven, thus retaining their vitamins and there are even microwave ovens with a steam option.

Cupboards and drawers

All kinds of practical cupboard and drawer storage arrangements are available to help you clear away your utensils and equipment tidily and logically. An empty corner is often usefully employed for a cooking pan carousel. The trend now is to use deep, wide drawers to store pans instead of cupboards. Drawers are much more convenient and orderly compared with cupboards, it is easy to pick out what you want and the whole space is fully used. Many kitchens are now fitted with a skirting-board tray: additional storage space a few centimetres in height or you could integrate this space into the drawers themselves, which makes them extra deep and roomy.

The floor

The kitchen floor often has to put up with a lot of wear and tear. Some areas will be used more intensively than others: you stand in front of a stove for longer than you do in front of a refrigerator. Consequently, flooring materials get worn away at different rates. If you have an open-plan kitchen, the room will look more spacious if you let the floor used, perhaps, for the living room continue through to the kitchen. Should you want to use a different material for the floor, remember that the area will appear bigger if you dispense with a separating strip where the two floor types meet. In theory, virtually all types of floor are suitable for use in kitchens, though a wooden floor does have the disadvantage of not being truly damp-proof.

Lighting

Kitchen lighting can be divided into two types. In addition to general basic lighting for illuminating the whole area, you will also need lighting directed over your hands when working at a kitchen surface. In other words, it is useful to have additional lighting fixed under wall-mounted cupboards or under shelving. Light from the ceiling is not suited to the task since you will often be standing in its path, casting a shadow over the spot where you are working. Remember to take into account the sort of impression that the lighting you choose will generate. White fluorescent strip-lighting can create very crisp shadows and make colours look a little pale; other types of strip-lighting are warmer. Halogen produces good light in general, and illuminates a work surface well. Halogen lights can be mounted on a tension cable, on a rail, or alternatively sunk into the base of a mounted cabinet.

Electricity sockets

Having lots of electricity sockets spread along the wall adjoining a work surface is no extravagance. Skirting courses containing cables can be mounted to the kitchen wall allowing the power point to be shifted along. Sockets do not have to be actually fixed to the wall: instead, you could have a recess at the back of the work surface containing movable sockets. Do not forget either that you must also have sockets for the refrigerator, oven, microwave and dishwasher; these must be accessible but not visible.

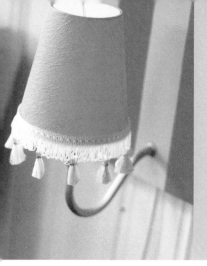

lighting

Two certainties about lighting: you need bright light to work by as well as lamps with a warm glow to create atmosphere. You need both kinds of lighting but how do you get the right balance? And how do you decide which lamp to choose and where to put it? For good lighting in the home you need to start off with a lighting plan.

The lighting plan

Attention given to lighting in a house often comes a poor second to everything else. Often it is only once the boxes have been unpacked that you start to think about where you are going to put your lamps. This is a pity because lighting is an important part of your decor and it is far better if it is integrated from the word go. If you are having a house built or are going to renovate one, it is wise to turn your thoughts to the lighting at a very early stage. If rooms are being ripped out and changed in an existing home it is a good idea to incorporate new lighting points for essential areas straightaway. Sketch a layout showing the position of the furniture in a room and where the electrical sockets are located, and also indicate where additional electrical sockets or lighting points are needed. You can show this lighting plan to a lighting specialist or electrician to make your requirements clear and to discuss the measures that will have to be taken.

Where should the electrical sockets go?

The standard rule is to have two electrical sockets in each corner of the room. If the distance between sockets is greater than 3.5 metres (12 ft), then have at least one double socket. This not only allows more room for lamp plugs, but also for occasional uses like the vacuum cleaner, for example. When thinking about electrical appliances, do not forget the television, video recorder, and telephone and computer connections. It will probably be useful to lead cables through to other rooms so you can phone from there, use the Internet or watch television.

Types of lighting

Basic general lighting ensures that the whole room is lit evenly. It is the sort of lighting that creates no shadows: in other words a ceiling light, 'up-lighters' (where a group of bulbs point upwards to the ceiling), spotlights directed at a white wall and wall-mounted lights. Work and spot lighting make it possible to see properly what you are doing: this may involve a spotlight or a reading lamp but could also include the strip-light under a kitchen cabinet. Atmospheric lighting creates a warm and cosy feeling in a room: for example a table lamp, standard lamp or strip-lighting to illuminate a painting.

General or work lighting can be changed to atmospheric lighting with a dimmer switch. If you need a bulb for a dimmer light, remember that energy-saving bulbs cannot be dimmed. Ordinary light bulbs and halogen lamps can be dimmed but cannot always share the same dimmer switches. A 12-volt halogen lamp cannot be dimmed using a normal light bulb dimmer switch, but the same switch can be used to dim a 220-volt halogen lamp. In fact, all three kinds of lighting (general/work/atmospheric) should be available in every room, although this does not mean that they all have to be used simultaneously.

The living room

The height at which lamps should be placed in the living room partly depends on the spot where the light is needed. Lighting for a sofa, for example, needs to be kept fairly low and creates an intimate mood at once.

TIP

Work lighting often produces a strong shadow against a wall. The shadow can be made to disappear, or at least be softened, by putting general lighting close to it, such as a standard lamp, for example.

A light above a table must be suspended 55–60 cm (20–24 in) from the table, otherwise you will be looking either at the lampshade or directly at the light source. It is recommended that, whatever you do, the lamps you have in a room be positioned at different heights for variety. It may be that you can dispense with a ceiling light or other kind of general lighting altogether if you find that several different light sources together perform the job just as well.

The bedroom

A bedroom also requires three kinds of light. As well as the bedroom being cosy (atmospheric lighting), it is important for you to be able to read in bed (work/spot lighting), while you also need adequate lighting to make the bed (general lighting). General lighting can be produced by two large suspended lamps next to the bed that also create atmosphere, by wall-mounted or ceiling lamps or an old-fashioned chandelier above the bed. Remember to position a reading lamp so it does not disturb a partner who is trying to sleep.

The kitchen

As well as having good general lighting (a ceiling lamp or lighting rail, for example), it is useful to have work lights under the kitchen cabinets. Other light sources can be positioned in addition to this to make the room cosier, such as glass-fronted cabinets that are lit from the inside.

The bathroom

In the bathroom, daylight is the best of all, of course. In the absence of any existing windows, you could introduce a dome light to the bathroom if the roof above is flat. If it is sloping, you could put in a skylight or dormer window. Otherwise, easily installed daylight systems are the latest thing on the market.

When installing general lighting do not forget your mirrors. Do not place lights too far away from mirrors and make sure that they are symmetrical. That way you avoid constantly standing in your own shadow and your face will be lit evenly. Bathrooms are damp by nature and require additional safety measures, so lights in bathrooms must be appropriate for that environment. Call in a registered electrician or lighting specialist for assistance if you are in any doubt.

Light bulbs, halogen lamps and energy-saving bulbs

Ordinary light bulbs provide a natural light. A matt-glass bulb emits light better than a clear-glass bulb. Clear-glass light bulbs, especially ornamental ones, are best used in transparent fittings. If the light from a bulb lacks sufficient warmth, you can change it for a flame or coloured-glass bulb. These diffuse soft light in shades of terracotta, yellow and jade. A warmly coloured lampshade can also perform miracles.

Halogen lamps emit twice as much light as ordinary bulbs with the same wattage and also last twice as long. They need to be fitted with transformers to convert mains voltage to low voltage. A halogen lamp produces a lot of heat and, consequently, must always be fitted with safety glass. Some halogen lamps are fitted with 'cold reflectors': they reflect the light forwards and the warmth backwards. Therefore, if you have built in halogen lamps to ceilings or walls, you must ensure there is enough free space surrounding them to absorb the heat emitted. Find out just how much space your particular halogen lamps require.

Energy-saving bulbs are available in a coiled, traditional or candle style. The traditional and candle styles are a little more expensive but do produce a warmer light. The greatest advantage of an energy-saving bulb is its long lifespan and low energy consumption. Just as with fluorescent strip-lighting, this makes them extremely appropriate for places where lights are kept switched on for long periods of time. Energy-saving bulbs cannot be dimmed, nor can they be connected to an electronic time switch, though they can be used with mechanical timers.

Outdoor lighting

If you place a lamp with a motion sensor next to the front door it will switch itself on every time someone approaches. This not only makes it easier to find the keyhole at night, but also wards off potential burglars. Do not put energy-saving bulbs in a motion-sensitive lamp because energy-saving bulbs need to warm up first. Moulded-glass lamps or bright halogen lamps are better: these produce plenty of bright light immediately. You can also buy lamps with built-in sensors that turn themselves on when it gets dark. Energy-saving bulbs can be used for this kind of lamp and would be the most economical choice for normal outdoor lighting that is on all night.

TIP

Always read the packaging when buying a light bulb. It will tell you the correct fitting for the bulb and the sort of light it produces, as well as the intensity of light. An energy-saving bulb of 11 watts produces just as much light as an ordinary light bulb of 60 watts. The lighting effect produced by spot light bulbs is also often shown.

windows

Dressed windows not only shield an interior but also serve to soundproof the indoors from the outdoors. Obviously, the most familiar format involves curtains. There are countless options open to you, even if you are just considering curtains, varying from transparent sari material to lined velvet.

Curtains

Choosing the type of curtains or the material to use depends on the size of the window. You can influence the impression made by a window simply by the way you hang or drape your curtains. A high window can be made to look lower by employing drapery or a pelmet, while long curtains used with small windows can suggest that the window reaches the floor as well. If radiators have been placed below windows, make sure that they can radiate their heat properly: curtains can be hung to a point just above a radiator, they can have a thin, translucent fabric attached at that point down to the floor, or the third possibility is not to line your curtains. It is preferable to choose the same design for your curtains in any one room, which creates a peaceful and unified look. Avoid small patterns if you have a large window; simple designs and natural fabrics tend to look better.

Ready-made curtains

There are many ready-made curtains and blinds in the shops these days, such as roller blinds, folding curtains and curtains fitted with eye-holes or loops. The advantage of ready-made curtains, of course, is that you can hang them up straightaway, although you may well have to hem them. A curtain with pleats or eye-holes is measured at twice the width of the window, which makes the material hang better.

Lining

Lining gives a curtain more volume. It also hides seams and hems and protects the curtain from the effects of (sun)light. Lining velvet curtains is far from extravagant because sometimes a little of the material loosens in the manufacturing process and can otherwise show up against the light as tiny holes.

Making your own curtains

There are various items available to help with making your own curtains, such as a strip you can stitch along the top of the curtain to create pleats. Or clips on which the curtain is hung, making immediate pleats. You can buy fixings for making eye-holes in the fabric, which are then pulled over a curtain rod or steel wire. Also there is a kind of adhesive tape that creates seams simply by ironing over it.

Amount of material

The amount of material you need depends on the kind of curtains you want. For pleated curtains, for example, you will need twice the length of the rail, multiplied by the length of the curtain. Do not forget to add to the calculation the material you use to make the hems: a generous hem looks best, so reserve at least 25 cm (10 in) extra (15 cm/6 in for the bottom and 10 cm/4 in for the top) for each length. If you have chosen a transparent material, you will need anything up to three times the length of the rail. Once you have hung curtains made from a heavier fabric, wait a few weeks for the material to straighten out properly before stitching the hems.

TIP

Curtains that are the perfect size should be dry-cleaned to avoid the danger of shrinkage. This applies to lined curtains in particular because different fabrics will shrink by different amounts. Material with a metallic structure should never come into contact with water because it may bubble and blister.

Hanging systems

You can hang curtains from a track, a pole or a steel wire. Poles come in wood, aluminium, plastic or metal, often with matching finials. Ensure that the thickness of the pole matches the style of the material. For an understated or classical look, choose a thin pole or a steel wire for flimsy voile or a similar light, gauzy fabric and use a track or a pole for heavier material, like velvet or lined curtains, but you can vary and contrast weights for a more dramatic effect.

If the window is particularly wide, it may be that standard-length poles are not available to fit it. You can buy poles fitted with screw threads at the ends to adjust the total length. If it is too long, the pole may start to bend in the middle, which can also happen if the curtain is too heavy. If this happens you must give the pole support in the centre.

A steel wire can be attached from a bracket either to the wall or the ceiling. It must be extremely well tensioned to prevent it buckling. If a wire is to be attached to a plaster wall, you must use special plasterboard plugs to prevent the wire from ripping itself out under the tension.

Curtain tracks come in a variety of materials. Aluminium tracks can be bent quite easily to make curves, making them useful for bay windows. The curtain header (the pleats at the top of the curtain) will conceal the rail.

TIPS

Indoor shutters can be obtained in a wooden louvred design. These can be painted any colour you like to suit your decor or else stained. Old-fashioned panelled shutters (which are one of the most effective methods of keeping light out of your room) can be custom-made by a carpenter to fit your windows.

Do you have a large area of curtain in which you want to make eye-holes? Find some specialists in making lorry tarpaulins or ships' sails. They will often have machinery that will do the job easily and saving you from a labour-intensive task.

It is possible to make curtains to fit even a round or triangular window: special curtain tracks are available.

Attic or conservatory windows

The majority of builders' merchants sell roller blinds for skylights, dormer and pivotal windows. Some manufacturers of skylights are also able to supply appropriate roller, pleated and blackout blinds which can be opened either by hand or with electric controls. Blackout blinds are backed with a layer of aluminium, which reflects back the sun's rays in summer but keeps warmth indoors in the winter.

Special systems are on sale for conservatories where (reflective) folding and pleated blinds following the slope of the glazing can be opened either by hand or electrically.

Roller blinds

Lined curtains may not always shut out the light and net curtains certainly will not. In these cases, additional roller blinds may offer the solution. If there is still an empty section of wall above the window, it will be possible to attach the roller blind from the ceiling instead of from the window frame, which will make the window appear higher.

A roller blind is usually pulled from the top downwards but can also be mounted on a windowsill and used as a valance to prevent anyone seeing in from outside without having to cover the entire window. Naturally, it must be possible to attach the blind to both sides of the window.

Panel blinds

Panel curtains are relatively new on the market. These are vertical lengths of material that can move forwards and backwards past each other – a kind of giant fabric Venetian blind. You can play with transparency by choosing different fabrics for the panels. The panels can be moved by hand or by means of electric controls. The latest development is to have three horizontal panels of material that can be pulled in front of and behind each other. For instance, three equally sized widths might cover a window from top to bottom. However, these widths can be moved independently of one another to leave the centre of the window free, for example, while also creating more colours and textures over your window.

Folding blinds

Folding blinds (Roman blinds, Austrian blinds) are usually the width of the window and are attached to a track by Velcro. A cord passes via the track to the back of the blind, which is pulled up in pleated folds when you pull on the cord. You can insert ribs into the blind to stiffen it and make it hang better. There are also folding blinds that are suitable for side-hung and cantilever windows. You can buy variants that let you

put two kinds of folding blind on one track: for example, a transparent blind for daytime and a lined blind at night.

There are sun blinds that can be pulled by a cord to produce pleats. These blinds are often fitted with a metallized layer that both reflects back sunshine and provides a good blackout.

Venetian blinds

Venetian blinds are sold in all kinds of widths and are made from all manner of materials: wood, plastics and aluminium. They are available in many colours and designs and can even come with a surrounding structure. One range has recently appeared on the market that reveals a design when closed. Venetian blinds can be installed in dormer windows and in side-hung and cantilever windows.

Venetian blinds can be bought ready-made and their size can be adjusted with the help of a pair of clippers especially for the purpose. Most can be assembled at home without the need for a professional. They are often extremely useful in bathrooms but note that wooden Venetian blinds can warp from steam or moisture in rooms where there is water.

Light filters

If you want to let the light in but do not want to be observed, you could consider putting sticky-backed plastic sheeting onto the windows. It is available in a variety of designs that give the window a sandblasted effect. If you would prefer not to use adhesives on the window, use chalk paper instead: large sheets are usually available from better copying shops or art suppliers. Attach the sheets to thin strips fixed to the top of the window frame.

You can also hang sheer fabric, muslin and voile, which will provide you with some privacy, filter out strong sunlight, but not block the all the light. Choose a patterned fabric that will create pretty shadows in your room. Or improvise with sari fabric for example to add a touch of exotic colour.

You can make so much more of your house just by getting the layout right. This will often do away with any need for serious renovation work. In many cases, just reorganizing a room or installing partition walls will be enough. A master bedroom can be turned into a study, the children's play corner can be integrated into the seating area and you can even create a brand-new room from the garage.

THE LIVING ROOM

The living room is the place in a home where we meet. Plus, where we do all kinds of things, such as watching television, reading, working and playing. Below are four ideas for the layout of a living room in which the interests of the family members have been taken into account. The premise is that we start with a living room measuring 5x6 m (16x20 ft), with access to the garden through French windows to the rear.

The piano/television room (1)

Although it can be a great bonus to have a piano in your living room, it can also get in the way. A piano is usually placed against a wall but, in this version, the piano occupies a central position in the room. A piece of furniture with a closed back has been placed against the back of the piano: this could be used for the television or stereo system. The piano and/or television cabinet create a cosy seating area together with the large L-shaped sofa and the armchair. There is a side-table with a reading lamp behind the sofa.

The reading corner (2)

If one person wants to watch television and another would rather read a book it is important for domestic harmony that neither one disturbs the other. This version features an L-shaped sofa, one end of which has no armrest. This creates a comfortable place for sitting, with an unobstructed view of the television next to the fireplace. Opposite, there is a swivel armchair that can be turned round so that someone reading a book is not bothered by the television.

Children's play area (3)

The children's play area is often located in the corner of the room or outside the seating area. In this version, however, the children have been given their own play area within the seating arrangement. At right angles to

the living room

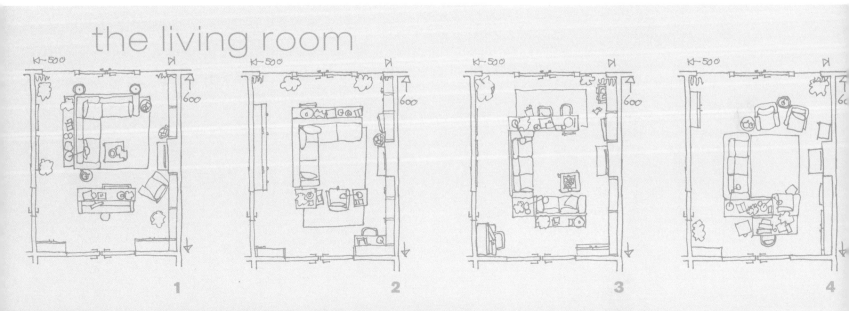

1   2   3   4

the three-seater sofa is a long, low table with two small chairs. Below it is a rug that demarcates the play area. It is still possible to get a good view of the garden from the sofa because the table is low and out of the field of vision. There is a piece of furniture next to the television for storing the children's toys and a side-table behind the two-seater sofa.

Computer corner (4)

This is an option if you like working in the living room or sitting at the computer and yet still want to feel involved with those relaxing in the seating area. The computer is on a small desk behind the armchair. If you do not want to look at the back of the computer you could put up a thin partition wall in between (of the notice-board type, for example). There is a long, low table placed next to the armchair. It is more attractive and harmonious if the desk and the low table are of the same design and/or material.

THE BATHROOM

The layout of the bathroom depends in part on the make-up of your household. If there are many of you living in one house and you need to leave home in a hurry, you do not want to have to wait your turn for the shower and brushing your teeth. It may be a good idea to give children their own bathroom that can also be used by guests.

Two showers (1)

Do you all need to leave home at the same time? In that case, a double shower may be the solution. It is also useful to have two separate washbasins that, in this version, have been attached to the two shower walls built to near ceiling height. The showers cannot be seen from the bath. It would look better if the shower areas were given separate lighting to make it clear that the room extends beyond the partition walls. Even with the extra fittings, there is still space over for a toilet next to the bath.

Two-in-one (2)

In this version, two separate bathrooms have been made out of one. The bathroom with the bathtub can be entered only from the master bedroom. There is also room here for a toilet, two washbasins side by side and a shower. The shower portrayed here has two glass panels, which enhance the feeling of space. The small bathroom (only 90 cm/3 ft wide) is for the children or guests (it can be reached from the hall). There is room inside for a toilet, a shower and a washbasin. Since the two rooms are next to each other, it will be simple to link up the plumbing, although you should ensure that water capacity will be sufficient when both showers are used at once.

Washing machine in the bathroom (3)

This layout is a useful solution if there is no option but to put the washing machine in the bathroom. In this version, the design keeps the machine as much out of sight as possible. It is behind a wall and can be reached through a door that also serves as a shower door when pulled shut. Two extendable mirrors have been mounted to the wall next to the double washbasins below the window.

Free-standing bath (4)

The bath in this large bathroom is free-standing, with one end set against a free-standing wall. This wall screens off the shower to the left and the toilet to the right. Washbasins have been placed either side of the entrance door with narrow mirrors above them and long shelves running next to them, thus creating a bathroom that can accommodate two people at once.

the bathroom

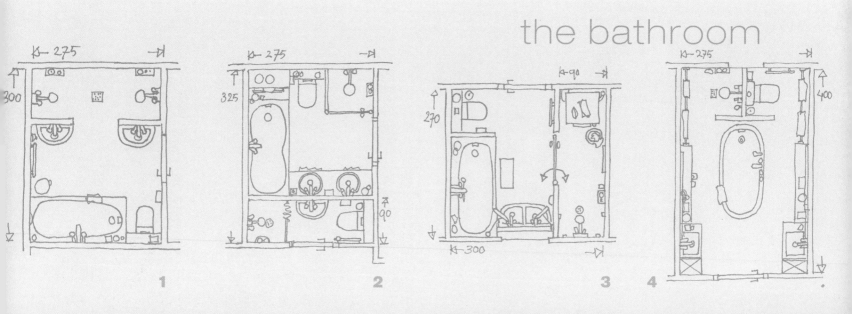

1   2   3   4

THE BEDROOM

The largest bedroom in the house is usually used by the parents. It often contains a double bed and a wardrobe, sometimes with space remaining for other pieces of furniture. The other bedrooms in the house are often much smaller and used as children's nurseries and guest rooms. However, the dimensions of the bedroom (that illustrated below being 4x4 m/13x13 ft) can often be utilized more efficiently, especially with the inclusion of a free-standing wall.

Parents' and baby's bedroom (1)

If a baby is sleeping in the parents' bedroom, a subdivision of the room can be made by means of a partition wall, in this version a high partition wall. Photographs and pictures can be put up on one side of the wall and a chest of drawers for the baby's clothes placed on the other side. There is room here, too, for the cot, changing mat and a comfortable armchair for the mother and baby.

Study for two (2)

The master bedroom previously described can be sacrificed if both of you need somewhere to work. In this instance, it has been decided to combine a study and a computer room in one. A half-height cabinet creates the partition itself, on which a television could be placed as well as providing office storage. This creates room for two desks, a side-table and a small two-seater sofa.

Television room and bedroom (3)

If you need another television room, it is often possible to create a good television corner in the master bedroom. A partition wall provides a good solution. The bed can be raised slightly so that storage drawers can be fitted underneath to make up for the loss of space.

A higher storage space has been placed at the foot of the bed in this version. A wall has been erected at the head of the bed at a height of approximately 150 cm (5 ft), and widened on top to create more surface space for lamps or other accessories. The space behind the partition makes a pleasant sitting area, while the television is on a shelf in an open section between two wardrobes with doors.

Double bedroom for children (4)

By handing over the largest bedroom to the children they will have not only a bedroom each but also a play area they can share. In this situation there is one entrance door from the hall or landing. A partition wall runs down the middle of the room, in the centre of which there are sliding doors, on either side of which a wardrobe and chest of drawers have been placed. The youngest child is probably best off in the rear bedroom because he or she will probably be the first to go to bed. One of the beds is an upper bunk bed with a small desk set underneath it. In the other room, the desk is at the head of the bed. You can sit in both rooms, either on a beanbag or in a little armchair, but during the day, by opening the sliding doors, you can create a large playroom for the children.

THE KITCHEN

The following kitchen layouts have been designed for three different people or for families. They are based on the premise of a house 6 m (20 ft) wide in which the kitchen is at the rear. The kitchen is placed against a wall measuring 3.5 m (11½ ft).

Professional kitchen (1)

If cooking is your hobby you will tend to spend a lot of time in the kitchen. This kitchen contains all the equipment and appliances you would need. A table has

the bedroom

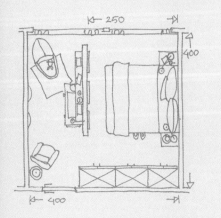

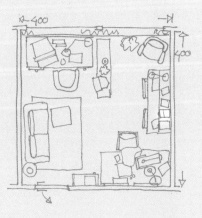

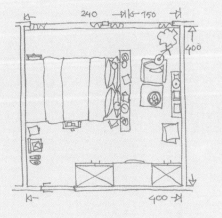

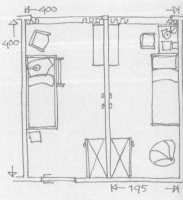

1   2   3   4

been built around the wide stove so that the cook can take part in the conversation while cooking. You could also use it as a breakfast bar or informal dining area. There is a large extraction hood above the stove. The kitchen is not visible from the living room but the dining area is.

Kitchen-diner (2)

A cooking island has been placed in the centre of the space containing the sink and cooking appliances. A shelf has been put up to the left of the cooking island for a small television. Against the left-hand wall, a unit has been placed in one corner for equipment such as the microwave and the refrigerator. In the other corner, another unit has space for a dishwasher. An upholstered bench has been inserted between the units, with cushions and a small table: the children will be able to enjoy watching television while the meal is being prepared. The dining table has been placed against the cooking island, which can also be used as extra preparation area. Behind the table, several low cupboards have been placed against the wall to store the crockery.

Kitchen hidden from sight (3)

Anyone sitting at the table in this kitchen will not feel that they are in a kitchen. The layout of this room is such that only cupboard doors are visible. The kitchen worktop containing the cooking appliances is set against the left wall. High cabinets fitted with doors stand either side of this. Opposite the worktop is the sink area (with storage space below it), enclosed by a wall with a height of about 2 metres (6½ ft). The layout maintains a feeling of spaciousness because the wall does not reach the ceiling. A table has been placed against the right-hand side of this wall, offering space for a computer or small television.

the kitchen

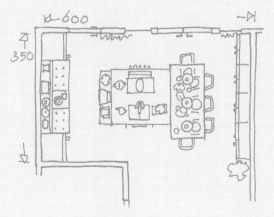

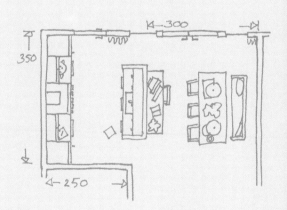

1

2

3

THE ATTIC

The attic can be very useful for storage but can also work as an extra room. Attic conversions can be quitre expensive and require architects and planning permission, but once completed, add invaluable living space and will also increase the value of your home. Children often adore the idea of sleeping and playing under the roof, but it can also make a comfortable bedroom, bathroom and study for their parents. An attic measuring 6x9 m (20x30 ft) has been assumed for the plans below.

Children in the attic (1)

Here the children have their own bedroom and their own entrance. They both have a bed, a desk and somewhere to sit. Two skylights have been put in the roof for one of them and a dormer window has been installed for the other, with the desk in front of it.

Relaxation room and laundry/work space (2)

Here the space has been split in two. At the top of the stairs you enter the laundry room, with the washing machine and dryer on either side of the desk. There is still space over for an ironing board and a cupboard has been constructed next to the stairs to store linen. A separate door closes off the boiler cupboard. The door in the partition wall leads to the relaxation area with a home gym. A sauna has been installed on the left with a shower attached; opposite the shower are a sunbed and two reclining chairs.

Parents in the attic (3)

The parents' bedroom can also be put in the attic. A large bedroom has been created with a desk or dressing table and an open-plan bathroom. There is space in the bathroom for a toilet, a shower, a bath and – in front of the dormer window – two washbasins.

the attic

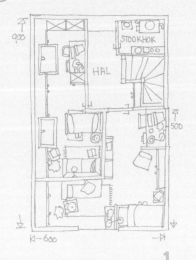

1

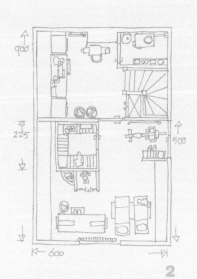

2

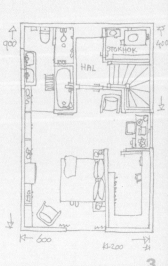

3

A low series of cabinets runs opposite the bed, among other things offering space for a television or you could build low shelves for books. Behind the bed is a 2 m (6½ ft) wide walk-in wardrobe with plenty of hanging space that can be closed with a sliding door.

THE GARAGE

Naturally, your garage was originally intended for parking the car and storing your bicycles and gardening and DIY equipment. However, with a few adjustments, you can turn the garage into an additional living space. Bringing some natural daylight and fresh air and ventilation into this room would be a great advantage, so look at the possibilities of installing a number of extra windows. Perhaps you could replace the garage door with a glass wall or a window. The garage in the examples below measures 4x6 m (13x20 ft).

Sports/fitness area (1)

The garage can be the ideal solution if you need somewhere for your fitness equipment or a table-tennis table. Here, the equipment has been placed in the centre of the room. Cupboards have been lined up against the two longer walls, with a clothes rack at the end so your sports clothing is to hand. There is a bench next to this for getting changed and alongside is a handy shower so you can freshen up immediately after exercise, and a deep cupboard.

Laundry/storeroom and workshop (2)

The washer-drier is often found in the garage sandwiched between the tools and paint pots. In this version, a wall has been inserted across the centre of the garage, with a door in the middle. The washing machine, drier and freezer are situated at the back of the room and there is also a work surface for folding up clothes. Deep cupboards have been created next to the

door for food or other storage. In the front room, there is space for a workbench and adjustable shelving units for paint and tools.

Solarium and garden shed (3)

This garage has been bisected as well, though there is no connecting door in this version, making the bicycle storage area accessible only from outdoors. The room containing the sunbed is reached from the main house, which means that you can access it in complete privacy. Additional cupboard space has been created next to the sunbed as well as a laundry area.

Separate bed-sitter (4)

The garage can offer the perfect solution to grown-up children who want to experiment with living on their own. You can create a separate entrance by replacing the garage door with window frames and a front-door frame. There is space in the room for a small sofa with a desk opposite. A high partition wall has been put up in the middle of the room. A cupboard with a television and some stereo equipment stands against one side of the seating area side of the room, while the bed is on the other side. The bed is therefore not visible from the seating area, creating the impression of a separate sleeping area. A reading lamp has been fixed to the wall and there is a wardrobe at the foot of the bed. A double sliding-door system has been incorporated 1 metre (3 ft) in front of the rear wall. A shower, toilet and kitchenette can all tucked away behind this. The door in the left wall links the bed-sitter to the rest of the house, to reassure anxious parents.

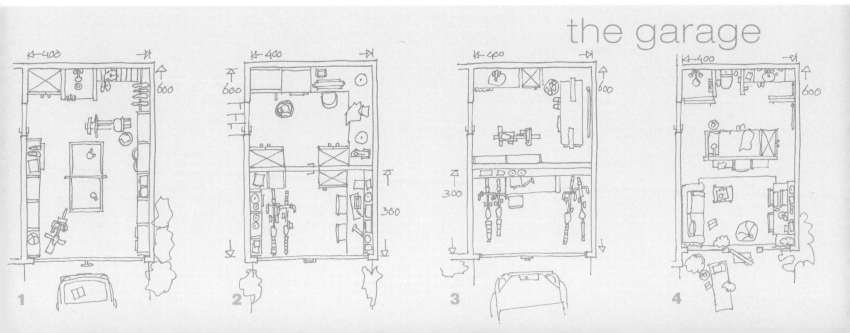

the garage

1 2 3 4

fireplaces and stoves

Curling up next to a fireplace with a warm drink and good book is one of the most relaxing and luxurious ways to spend an evening. Nowadays, even if you don't have a functioning flue you can still create the same effect with gas burners and electric appliances. Even more conveniently, the latest fires burn smokeless gel.

Key questions

A number of things are important when buying a fireplace or stove. One of the most vital questions is: do I have a flue? If you do, does it still work properly? If you don't, where is the right place to put one in? Another important consideration is whether the fire or stove is intended merely to create a pleasant atmosphere, or whether it has to function as a source of extra heating as well. Additionally, you will need to decide whether you want a fire that can be turned on and off quickly and easily (gas appliances) or something that can take a little more time (wood-burners). As far as designs are concerned, the choice is virtually unlimited.

Fireplace or stove?

Nowadays, many stoves — theoretically intended to be heaters — have an increasingly attractive appearance and some fireplaces — still valued more for character than for anything else — can produce a high level of heat. The difference between them is no longer as clear as it once was. Nonetheless, it generally holds true that a stove is free-standing, while a fireplace is usually built into a wall. A stove is usually a closed unit, although most models have a large, glass window. Fireplaces are not fuelled only by firewood these days: there are also 'character' fireplaces that burn gas or even gel. Stoves can be fuelled by either wood or gas.

The traditional fireplace

A traditional fireplace usually has a brick or stone base onto which firebricks can be placed and then the fire laid on top of these. Alternatively a grate can be used instead to contain logs. An ashpan below the grate collects fallen ash and debris. There should be a fireproof casing, made of firebricks, brick or a ceramic material, either behind or surrounding the grate. There should also be a hood above the grate to collect the smoke and funnel it into the flue. The hood is usually hidden behind a mantelpiece, which determines the appearance of the fireplace.

Built-in and insert fireplaces

A built-in fireplace is made of a metal box that is built into the wall. The flue is often built-in as well so that, in fact, only the front of it is visible. This can be camouflaged with a mantelpiece, which can be custom-made if necessary.

An insert fireplace is made of a sheet-steel or cast-iron box that is put straight into an opening, such as the existing opening for a fireplace. In appearance, an insert fireplace is much like the built-in version.

Protruding, hanging and free-standing fireplaces

Fireplaces can also be placed in front of a wall or even suspended on a wall, free of the floor: they usually have rather eye-catching designs. A fireplace can also be placed in the middle of a room: free-standing. This fireplace island and the hood are often made from the same material. Although the flames from such a fire are visible from all angles, its heat yield is low.

Soapstone and tiled stoves

If the exterior of a stove has been tiled or covered with soapstone, it will continue to give out heat, even when no longer burning fuel, for a few hours more (sometimes even up to 12 hours!). Gas-burning versions of these stoves are also available.

Wood-burners

A fireplace or stove that burns wood also smells pleasant and crackles comfortingly. If you are burning wood just for decorative purposes, a fireplace radiates back 10–20 per cent of the heat produced. A fireplace that can be closed (for instance, with a glass screen) can return up to 60 per cent of the heat produced. In such a situation, it is often possible to direct this heat to other rooms in the house via additional conduits. These days, there are advanced stoves equipped with sensory devices that monitor combustion and control airflow. This produces the maximum return from the fire and limits the amount of harmful combustion gases.

Gas-burners

Stoves and fireplaces can also be fuelled by gas. Turning the fire on and off is easy: you either open the gas pipe or simply press a button, and sometimes you can even use remote control. A new system has just come onto the market, known as the closed combustion system, that makes it possible to have a gas-fuelled fireplace without the need for a flue. A simple roof or exterior-wall outlet is sufficient.

Electric fireplaces

An electric fireplace needs no outlets at all. These appliances can be placed anywhere. The flames are not real and are produced as a two-dimensional glow on a screen. However, electric fireplaces are not simply for looking at; they also emit heat that you can regulate. They can sometimes even blow out cool air. Electrical appliances are cheaper than gas- and wood–burners, and take up less space as well.

Gel-burners

Fireplaces fuelled by gel are relatively new. Gel produces scarcely any smoke at all. The gel is in a small container that, if desired, can be placed among artificial logs in the fireplace. Special fireplaces are available for this kind of gel heating.

Flue or exterior-wall outlet?

Whether you need a flue or not depends on your combustion system. There are two options. The oxygen needed by a fire in a fireplace comes from the room it is in. The waste gases it produces are transported away to the outside via a conduit, such as is the case for a wood-burning fireplace. Since oxygen is being removed from the room, it is vitally important for the room to be well ventilated, especially in houses with good insulation and double glazing. In a closed-combustion system, the oxygen necessary for combustion is obtained from outside, thus requiring a double-walled pipe with an outlet on the exterior of the house. The pipe's outer ring introduces oxygen to the fire, while the inner pipe expels the waste gases. This pipe does not need to run to the crest of the roof but may also protrude from the side of the building. This makes it possible to put fireplaces like these in flats. The closed system is only possible for closed gas-fuelled appliances.

A flue will be necessary for wood-burning fireplaces and some gas appliances: open-combustion systems. If your house already has a flue, have a specialist decide whether it still complies with today's standards and requirements. An old flue may be damaged and, as a result, no longer functional, even if it has never been used! This particularly applies to flues dating from 1975 or before. If the flue is still in working order, have a professional decide whether its diameter is adequate for your purposes.

The chimney

It is important to insulate the flue because the temperature from waste gases can rise to 900°C (1652°F). However, insulation is also important to achieve a good thermal draw. The flue expels waste gases through the chimney, which may run up the side of a detached house. Beware, building a new chimney can take some time, and a new fireplace may sometimes only be used for the first time anything up to six weeks after completion.

The mantelpiece

The mantelpiece frames the fireplace and, consequently, catches the eye. They can be minimalist – a clean design made from marble or stone or an ornate centrepiece. You can also adorn the top of the mantelpiece with photographs, postcards or small collections of found objects.

The customary materials used for mantelpieces are wood and stone. If you want a stone-faced mantelpiece, you can choose from limestone, marble and granite. A limestone mantelpiece is usually cheaper than one made from marble but the material is also more delicate. Limestone is light in colour and often comes from France or Portugal. Wooden mantelpieces are usually made from pine or mahogany. You can also buy do-it-yourself versions in MDF from builders' merchants. Modern mantelpieces can be made from steel, copper or brass.

TIP

The flue should be cleaned at least once a year. Not doing this increases the risk of chimney fires and reduces the draw needed for good combustion. Many insurance companies require proof that the flue has been regularly maintained where the cause of damage involves the fireplace.

Following a period in which greys and whites were interior design's favourites, it is time again for an exuberant palette of colour. Read here about what colours can do and how you can manipulate contrasting cool and warm tones to your advantage.

Colour and space

Colour can strongly influence not only the character of a space but also how it is perceived. A room painted in dark colours looks smaller than the same room painted in lighter tones. To arrive at a suitable choice, not only should you look at the properties of a colour but also consider the light entering a room and the number of windows. In a room with few windows your best option would be a colour that looks good by artificial light.

A colder light will enter a room if it faces north and it will benefit from the use of warm colours to make it feel cosier and warmer. Conversely, a south-facing room with white walls will reflect the light, which can make the room too bright. Very bright colours are emphasized by sunlight, enhancing their strength. Pastels are therefore better suited to south-facing rooms for that reason.

Optical illusions

Rooms look cosy when painted red or yellow. Reddish-violet, reddish-orange, orange, orange-yellow and yellow make rooms smaller. These colours are particularly appropriate for rooms facing north that never get direct sunlight. Be careful about small rooms if you have decided on dark red: the walls may appear to force themselves in on you. Red is sometimes best used as a detail, for instance as a section of colour above a table. If a room has to look larger, use cooler colours such as violet, blue, blue-green, green or colours with a lot of white in them. Cool colours are suitable for south- and west-facing rooms. Shades of peach lend light and space to a room.

A coloured ceiling can make a room more intimate but the use of too imposing a colour can have an oppressive effect. A white ceiling reflects 10–15 per cent more light than a ceiling painted in a colour. A room will appear higher if you avoid painting the walls in one colour all the way to the ceiling but, instead, stop about 25 cm (10 in) short. You can create the same effect by painting the wall in vertical stripes. Horizontal stripes will make the room appear wider.

Colour combinations

Colours can influence each other. The combinations of red-green, yellow-purple and orange-blue constitute the starkest possible contrasts: they enhance each other. In other words, if you want your interior to be colourful but not too restless, do not go for contrasting colours but choose accents from just one colour instead: the principal component colours from which a colour is made. This depends on the colours that have been mixed. For instance, yellow can tend towards green (in which case there is more blue in it); conversely, it can tend towards orange (in which case there is more red in it). If you employ different shades of one chief colour in a room, you will make it even calmer. Adding white creates the most restful colour shades. Warm colours, such as yellow and red, are more intense than a cool colour such as blue. A wall painted red closes in on you far more than the same wall in blue. The more colours are mixed, the more their intensity is changed. A warm, green colour is produced when blue is mixed with a great deal of yellow and this is much more intense than the original blue.

TIP

Instead of deciding to paint a room in a combination of contrasting colours, you could also choose colours that share the same intensity. Its dynamism will then be created in its unity of colour, materials and textures.

storage

It is easier to find things in a tidy house. Having enough space to store things will give you more space for living your life and enjoying your home.

Creating space

You do not have to start renovating your house in order to create space. First, you should examine your rooms closely: are they being used as effectively as possible? Consider, for instance, the space under or below the stairs or bed. And is the furniture taking up unnecessary space? In some cases, it may be better to use a pull-out table.

The bedroom

Reconsider whether the bedrooms really suit the people who use them. Children usually have a lot of toys and so on, but are often given the smallest rooms. It may be more practical to let the children have the master bedroom and make it double up as a playroom as well. You can create a lot of extra storage space in a children's room if you have a raised bed, for example, with a desk or chest of drawers below it.

Storing clothes

Wardrobes need a depth of at least 60 cm (2 ft) for the clothes hangers. If there is no room for a cupboard of this size, you can hang clothes on short (preferably extendible) rods that extend outwards. If you do not have much width to work with, but you do have the depth, you could choose a carousel wardrobe. The clothes hang on a rail and an electric motor causes the entire contents to move along in rotation before your eyes. A wardrobe lift is another option if the room has a high ceiling. It contains a rod on which you hang your clothes. This rod is fixed high up in the wardrobe but can be pulled forwards and downwards.

Screening

Items on shelves do not always have to be visible. A curtain can hide 'mess'. If you have a lot of transparent items on shelves, such as glassware, a voile curtain can create an attractive effect. Apart from curtains, sliding doors are an ideal way to conceal things.

Organizing

Make sure that the things you need most often are easily accessible. If it turns into an ordeal every single time that you go to get the vacuum cleaner out of the cupboard, it is either the storage place that is wrong or else the organization inside the cupboard. Something is also amiss if you continually need to use a stepladder to get to what you want. Organize objects according to how much they get used. Whatever is used least can be stored a little further away or higher up. Items used seasonally can also change position. Wellington boots and thick coats can be at the front in the winter but in summer it will be the inflatable paddling pool. Remember though: things that are out of sight are often out of mind.

Doors

Whether or not a piece of furniture devoted to storage is practical also depends on its design. One with hinged doors will take up more space than one with a roller door. There are also folding doors (which take up half the space of hinged doors), hinged doors that fold inside a cabinet (which, like a roller door, is useful for hiding a television), sliding doors (though they only give you access to half the storage space), a foldaway door (useful for high cupboards), a swing-shut door (a foldaway door that is pushed back into the cabinet) and a table flap (which opens downwards to create a stable desktop).

Castors and hoists

Storage furniture becomes flexible and movable as soon as you attach wheels to the bottom. For instance, you could put pull-out cupboards under the stairs, but ensure you protect wooden floor surfaces from castors. Pulleys provide excellent assistance for storing things, such as a bicycle in a hallway.

architectural salvage

What captures the character and atmosphere of the past better than the design, the details and the materials of that time? Fortunately, historical architectural materials are still widely available — anything from authentic panelled doors to classic fireplaces to real antique tiles — which you can find at salvage yards, house sales and antique merchants. And if these do not quite meet our modern standards, there are plenty of replicas available that can also be custom-made.

Original details

If you have bought an old house it is quite likely that bits of modernization have been done. Over the course of time original details may well have been destroyed or removed, but with luck you may find that they have only been 'concealed'. In the 1970s, 'modernization' seemed to be all about covering up panelled doors with sheets of hardboard and hiding beautifully moulded ceilings behind panel-system ceilings. With this in mind, take a careful look at your home and see whether any original details still remain that can be salvaged. Missing or replacement parts can very often be found quite cheaply from a dealer in architectural salvage.

If you are planning to renovate a house using salvaged materials or to integrate salvaged items when building a new house, you would be well advised to choose a builder or architect with experience of these things. To reuse salvage materials in a modern context can require extra care and attention since dimensions will not be standard ones of today and work will require a customized approach. For that reason, it sometimes makes more sense to purchase salvage items first and only make the layout drawings afterwards.

Customizing

It is often no problem if the dimensions of, for instance, a door or doorframe are not exactly right. The majority of salvage dealers have a workshop where items can be customized to fit or where they can be restored. Some dealers will also deliver salvage items to your door and install them for you. Do you want a particular door or mantelpiece? If so, make a good note of the measurements and put any designs on paper.

Old or aged?

There is a difference between old and aged salvage materials. Old materials are genuinely old, maybe even antique, and have a history, while aged materials have a well-used look only because they have been treated in a way that ages them attractively; sometimes, they can even be more expensive! Aged materials are often in standard sizes and can be found everywhere. There is more of a problem, however, when it comes to old materials. These be more difficult to find and are often not in standard sizes. Only a real professional will be able to work with them. Decent aged versions of old materials are available in shops: facing bricks, panelled doors, natural stone, wall and floor tiles, staircases and newel posts, bathroom fittings and fixtures, mantelpieces and parquet floors.

Origin

Old construction and decorative materials come from old houses that have been renovated or demolished, possibly from Europe as well as the UK. A dealer buys these materials from the demolition contractor or direct from the owner. If you buy a mantelpiece from a dealer, it may be that the mantelpiece is merely a composite from various models that were all missing something. Consequently, if you are buying a salvage item, make sure that it is genuinely complete. This is easiest to see if it has been put on display in the shop. Several factors determine the price of the material: its rarity and the relative degree of supply and demand. The rarer the product, the higher the price.

Stained glass

Many stained-glass windows were removed in the 1970s, in particular because they could not be combined with double-glazing techniques.

Dealers still have plenty of stained-glass windows in stock. It is not easy, however, to fit an old stained-glass window into an existing opening because you will need to have the exact size. A stained-glass window can be hung in front of an existing window, or else framed: ideal for spots where you do not want people to be able to look in. Did your house once have stained-glass windows but you don't know what they looked like? Take photographs of stained-glass windows in similar houses to yours in the neighbourhood: a stained-glass studio will probably be able to make you a new window when you show them these. Nowadays, stained glass can be inserted between two panes of glass without any problems with the double glazing. A recent idea is a window screen made from steel and stained glass: the steel frame creates a strong support structure that also deters burglars.

Bathroom fixtures and fittings

A bath with feet or an characterful old kitchen or bathroom tap can sometimes still be found at a dealer's. As the baths are not new, they often need to be repainted or re-enamelled first. Some dealers will do this for you for an additional fee, allowing you to choose the colour and even the design. Do remember that an old bathtub is often heavier than contemporary models and your floor must be able to bear the load. From the point of view of hygiene, also check that old bathroom fixtures or tiles have no cracks in them, apart, that is, from the aged craquelé effect, which you can ignore. Replica baths are also available if you do not want an old bath but want one that echoes the past. When buying a tap, make sure that it has been checked and, if needs be, discuss with the installer whether the tap you have chosen can indeed be used in your home.

Floors

Old parquet that is in relatively good condition is generally quite hard to find. New parquet that has been given an attractive, deliberately aged look, however, is far more widely available. Floorboards are available everywhere. They are sometimes sawn from old beams from railway carriages, manor houses in France or cheese-maturing shelves in Dutch cheese warehouses. Stone floors often come from castles or great mansions. Burgundian valley stone or limestone slabs were sometimes as much as 8x20 cm (3x8 in) thick but are now sawn into several layers, with the uppermost the most expensive. The age of marble can be guessed from its base: marble with a chiselled base was extracted before 1900, while marble with a sawn base dates from 1900 or later. Antique floor tiles can still be obtained if you search hard enough and it is certainly worth the effort as good copies are virtually impossible to find. Make sure you know how to look after these tiles properly though.

TIPS

If an old door has to be given a fresh coat of paint, it may be necessary to remove all the old layers first. Instead of using a paint scraper and risking damage to the wood, you can also get a professional company to treat the door with a caustic solution (lye). This will remove all the layers of paint without causing any damage or loosening any glued joints.

Genuine antique tiles can be quite difficult to distinguish from new 'antique' copies. Age can sometimes be evidenced by a residue of cement on the back and by irregularity of shape. The indentations in the corners are other features that betray age. Before the tiles were cut, the original mould contained two small nails to prevent the tiles from slipping. Very early versions display an indentation in each corner.

This gives a taste of interiors suppliers and their products, while providing sufficient information for following up individual ideas. A full spectrum has been included: from budget to traditional to designer. Street addresses are given in cases where the customer is likely to visit the shop or premises. Mail order features prominently, while web sites can be a very useful and illuminating resource.

An Angel at my Table
116A Fortress Road,
London NW5 2HL/
14 High Street, Saffron Waldon, Essex CB10 1AY
020 7424 9777/
01799 528777
furniture and accessories with French country feel: light, pretty, well priced

Bhs
020 7262 3288 for stores
chain store famous for lighting; attractive homeware range

Böbeck Knight
0870 013 3115 for mail order
furniture and accessories with a sharp modern feel

Cargo HomeShop
0870 2410304 for stores
informal budget homeware

Colefax and Fowler
110 Fulham Road,
London SW3 6RL
020 7244 7427
traditionally English fabrics, wallpapers, accessories

The Conran Shop
Michelin House,
81 Fulham Road,
London SW3 6RD
020 7589 7401
www.conran.com
furniture and accessories with strong design input

The Cotswold Company
0870 550 2233 for mail order
www.cotswoldco.com
extensive range of contemporary furniture and accessories

Designers Guild
267–271 King's Road,
London SW3 5EN
020 7243 7300
www.designersguild.com
modern fabric designs, paints, wallcoverings

Fired Earth
117–119 Fulham Road,
London SW3 6RL
and branches
01295 814300
www.firedearth.com
V&A historic paint range, wall/floor tiles, rugs

Grimes & Co
00 353 1806 8918
www.grimesco.ie
quirky furniture and accessory designs: simple wood and pretty textiles

Habitat
0845 6010740 for stores
www.habitat.net
legendary furniture/interiors shop and design pioneers

Igloo
0800 068 19100
www.igloo.co.uk
range of furniture and accessories with bold modern design

IKEA
020 8208 5600
www.ikea.com
Swedish superstores with economical and innovative furniture and accessories

Laura Ashley
01686 622116 for branches
www.laura-ashley.com
fabrics, paints, tiles, wallcoverings

Liberty
210–220 Regent Street,
London W1R 6AH
020 7734 1234
www.liberty-of-london.com
fabrics (inc. famous Liberty prints), furniture, linens, rugs, chinaware, accessories

McCord
0870 908 7005 for mail order
www.mccord.uk.com
range of furniture and accessories: modern with classic touch

Muji
020 7792 8283 for stores
simple furniture, storage and accessories in Japanese minimalist style

Next Home
0845 6007000
www.next.co.uk
paints, wallcoverings, accessories

Ocean
0870 8484840 for mail order
www.oceancatalogue.com
range of furniture and accessories: modern simplicity

Oka Direct
0870 160 6002 for mail order
www.okadirect.com
range of furniture and accessories with distinct Asian flavour: much bamboo and rattan

Osborne & Little
304 King's Road,
London SW3 5UH
020 7352 1456
www.osborneandlittle.co.uk
fabrics, wallcoverings, accessories in classic English style

The Pier
200 Tottenham Court Road, London W1P 7PL
020 7814 5020 for mail order
www.pier.co.uk
furniture (esp. wicker) and accessories, with ethnic flavour

Shaker
72–73 Marylebone High Street, London W1
020 7935 9461
www.shaker.co.uk
collection of furniture and accessories in restrained Shaker style

BUILDING AND DECORATING

B&Q
020 8 466 4166 for stores
www.diy.com
multiple DIY superstores

Homebase
0645 801800 for stores
www.homebase.uk
multiple DIY superstores

FLOORS

Allied Carpets
0800 192192
www.alliedcarpets.com
multiple carpet and wooden floor superstores

Alma Home
12–14 Greatorex Street,
London E1 5NF
020 7377 0762
www.almahome.co.uk
leather furnishings, floor- and wallcoverings

Amtico
0800 667766
www.amtico.com
high-quality vinyl flooring: known for faux marble/wood/tile effects

Axminster Carpets
01297 32244
www.axminster-carpets.co.uk
long-established name in British wool carpets

Bill Amberg
10 Chepstow Road,
London W2 5BD
020 7727 3560
leather flooring

Bisazza
020 8640 7994
terrazzo flooring

Brintons
01562 820000
www.brintons.net
range of wool-based carpets

Casteinau Tiles
175 Church Road,
London SW13 9HR
020 8741 2452
stone, slate, terracotta, ceramic tiles

Criterion Tiles
196 Wandsworth Bridge Road, London SW6 2UF
020 7736 9610
www.criterion-tiles.co.uk
ceramic and terracotta tiles at good prices

Easternglazed
01603 423391
www.i-i.net/easternglazed
slate, terracotta, limestone, marble and ceramic tiles

H&R Johnson
01782 575575
www.johnson-tiles.com
range of ornamental tiles

Junkers
01376 517512
hardwood strip floors

Kahrs UK
01243 778747
www.kahrs.se
wood strip, parquet and mosaic flooring

Liberon Waxes
01797 367555
wood dyes/waxes/sealants, marble treatments

Marlborough Fine English Tiles
01672 512422
ceramic tiles

Mosaic Workshop
Unit b, 443–449
Holloway Road,
London N7
020 7 263 2997
mosaic floors

Natural Flooring Direct
0800 454 721 for mail order
wool, coir, jute, sisal, seagrass floor coverings

Naturestone
01344 627617
www.stone.co.uk
flooring of limestone, sandstone, slate and quartz

Pergo
01608 646222
www.pergo.com
laminate flooring

Philip & Tacey
01264 332171
www.philipandtacey.co.uk
handpainted tiles

Reject Tile Shop
178 Wandsworth Bridge
Road, London SW6 2UQ
020 7731 6098
www.criterion-tiles.co.uk
well known for good
seconds and ends of lines

Ryalux Carpets
01706 716000
www.carpetinfo.co.uk
wool and synthetic carpets

Saraband Designs
01453 872579
www.saraband-
designs.co.uk
flooring made from wool,
seagrass, sisal, coir and
jute

Stone Age
020 7385 7954
www.stone-age.co.uk
stone for walls and
floors

Tarkett-Sommer
01905 795004
wooden flooring

Tiles of Stow
01608 658993
www.tilesofstow.co.uk
hand-decorated tiles

Wicanders
01403 710002
cork flooring

World's End Tiles
Old British Railways
Yard, Silverthorne Road,
London SW8 3HE
020 7819 2100
www.worldsendtiles.co.uk
varied and extensive
range of tiles for walls
and floors

WALLS
for tiles, see under
floors, above

3M
www.3m.com
huge variety of
practical/industrial
products, including
masking tape used when
painting

Auro
01799 543077
www.auroorganic.co.uk
traditional/organic
paints, stains, oils, waxes

Craig & Rose
01383 740000
paints, inc. historic
colours, distemper

Farrow & Ball
249 Fulham Road,
London SW3 6HY
01202 876141 mail
order/stockists
www.farrow-ball.com
National Trust historic
paint range

**Nutshell Natural
Paints**
01364 73801 for mail
order
distemper with natural
pigments

Paint Magic
48 Golborne Road,
London W10 5PR
020 8960 9960
paint, coloured
distemper, other paint
products

Sanderson
01895 830000
www.sanderson.co.uk
period paints and
wallcoverings

FURNITURE

Amazing Emporium
249 Cricklewood
Broadway,
London NW2 6NX
020 8208 0704
www.amazingemporium
.com
huge showroom of beds
and dining suites in
quality woods

Blue Door Yard
74 Church Road,
London SW13 0DG
020 8748 9785
furniture in Swedish
Gustavian style

Divani
01685 844444 for mail
order
sofas and armchairs in
contemporary designs,
with a range of covers

Harvey Baker Design
01803 521515
www.harvey-baker-
design.co.uk
ready-to-paint MDF
furniture

Heal's
196 Tottenham Court
Road, London W1 7LQ
020 7636 1666
www.heals.co.uk
long-established
furniture store with
reputation for quality and
design

**The Iron Bed
Company**
01243 778999
www.ironbed.com
range of elegant metal
beds

Knoll International
1 Lindsay Street,
London EC1 9PQ
020 7236 6655
www.knollint.com
contemporary furniture
with strong design, also
classic chairs

Leather Workshop
01495 243000 for mail
order
leather sofas and
armchairs in
contemporary designs

Odeon
01495 717170 for mail
order
modern design in sofas
and armchairs, range of
covers

Purves & Purves
220–224 Tottenham
Court Road,
London W1T 7QE
020 7580 8223
www.purves.co.uk
high-profile new design
of furniture and
accessories

Ron Arad Associates
62 Chalk Farm Road,
London NW1 8AN
020 7284 4963
thoughtful modern
furniture, often metal

SCP
135–139 Curtain Road
EC2
020 7739 1869
www.scp.co.uk
works with current big
names in furniture
design, also relaunches
classic pieces

Scumble Goosie
01453 731305
ready-to-paint MDF
furniture

Thomas Lloyd
01443 771333 for mail
order
contemporary designs in
leather sofas and
armchairs, echoing the
company's traditional
range

Vitra
30 Clerkenwell Road,
London EC1M 5PG
020 7608 6200
www.vitra.com
long-term manufacturer
of the Eames' furniture,
also other classic designs

ANTIQUES/CLASSICS/
RETRO

After Noah
121 Upper Street,
London N1 1QP
020 7359 4281
www.afternoah.com
restored furniture and
accessories

**Alfie's Antique
Market**
13–25 Church Street,
London NW8 8DT
020 7723 6066
www.alfies.com
vast number of dealers
and wide range of
antiques

CC41/Sam Walker
27 Shorts Gardens,
London WC2H 9AP
020 7240 7800
design classics, esp.
chairs, also kitchenware

Century
68 Marylebone High
Street, London W1U 5JH
020 75100
American classic and
contemporary furniture

CO2
Unit 90, Stables Market,
Chalk Farm Road,
London NW1
020 7609 0857
classic modern and
contemporary furniture

Fandango
50 Cross Street,
London N1 2BA
020 7226 1777
www.fandango.uk.com
concentrates on classic
European furniture from
the 60s

The French House
125 Queenstown Road,
London SW8 3RH
020 7978 2228
www.thefrenchhouse
.co.uk
French furniture, esp.
beds, from 18th/19th
centuries

Planet Bazaar
149 Drummond Street,
London NW1 2PB
020 7387 8326
www.planetbazaar.co.uk
mainly 60s classic
furniture, esp. chairs,
plus vintage
lighting

Portobello Road
Antiques Market
Portobello Road,
W10/W11
020 7229 8354
www.portobelloroad.co.uk
biggest antiques market
in London and huge
variety of stalls

BATHROOM

Aston Matthews
141–147a Essex Road,
London N1 2SN
020 7226 7220
www.astonmatthews
.co.uk
bathroom fixtures and
fittings, radiators

Bisque
244 Belsize Road,
London NW6 4BT
020 7328 2225
www.bisque.co.uk
radiators and heated
towel-rails

Burge & Gunson
13–27 High Street,
London SW19
extensive range of
bathroom fixtures,
fittings, radiators and
accessories,
plus jacuzzis

C.P. Hart
020 7902 1040 for
brochure
www.cphart.co.uk
designer bathrooms (and
kitchens)

Chadder & Co
01342 823243
www.chadder.com
antique and traditional
bathroom fixtures and
fittings

**The Heated Mirror
Company**
01666 84003
heated mirrors that don't
steam up

M.C. Stone
69 Goldney Road,
London W9 2AR
020 7289 7102
www.mcstone.co.uk
minimalist bathrooms
featuring stone, marble,
granite, slate or mosaics

Pipe Dreams
72 Gloucester Road,
London SW7 4QT
020 7225 3978
www.pipedreams.co.uk
luxury custom-designed
bathrooms, plus jacuzzis
and steam showers

Radiating Style
020 8577 9111
www.radiatingstyle.co.uk
designer radiators,
mostly European

**Villeroy & Boch
Bathrooms**
020 8871 4028
bathroom fixtures and
fittings

West One Bathrooms
45–46 South Audley
Street London W1K 2PY
020 7499 1845
www.westonebathrooms
.com
large showroom
displaying exclusive
designer bathrooms

KITCHEN

Aga-Rayburn
01952 642000 for
stockists
iconic kitchen ranges
for a variety of fuels

Bosch
01908 328200 for
stockists
ultra-efficient kitchen
appliances

Bulthaup
020 7495 3665
calm, minimalist
kitchens, with much
stainless steel

Ceramica Blue
10 Blenheim Crescent,
London W11 1NN
020 7727 0288
www.ceramicablue.co.uk
surprising range of
ceramics from around
the world

Cucina Direct
0870 727 4300 for mail
order
www.cucinadirect.co.uk
extensive kitchenware
catalogue

David Mellor
4 Sloane Square,
London SW1W 8EE
020 7730 4259
high-quality kitchen and
tableware

Divertimenti
139–141 Fulham Road,
London SW3 6SD
020 7581 8065
comprehensive range of
kitchen- and tableware

GEC Anderson
01442 846999 for
catalogue
stainless-steel kitchens,
work surfaces and sinks

Miele
01235 554455 for
stockists
www.miele.co.uk
appliances for an
efficient kitchen

Neff
01908 328328 for
stockists
high-design, high-
performance kitchen
appliances

Poggenpohl
01908 247600 for
stockists
restrained luxury
German kitchens

Reject China Shop
183 Brompton Road,
London SW3 1NU
020 7581 0739
www.chinacraft.uk
bargains in more formal
chinaware ranges

Siematic
01438 369327 for
stockists
elegantly efficient
kitchens and appliances

Smeg
0870 8437373
www.smeguk.com
industrial-design
kitchens and
appliances

Stone Masters
020 8566 8222
kitchen worktops (and
floors, bathrooms,
fireplaces) in granite,
marble, slate, limestone

Thomas Goode
19 South Audley Street,
London W1K 2NU
020 7499 2823
www.thomasgoode.co.uk
long-established mecca
for fine china, glass and
silver; some designer
lines

LIGHTING

Christopher Wray
591–593 King's Road,
London SW6 2YW
020 7751 8701
www.christopher-wray
.com
celebrated traditional
lighting shop, now
featuring modern
designs too

Designer Light Shop
4 Kennington Road,
London SE1 7BL
020 7928 0097
contemporary lights by
big-name European
designers

Focus Gallery
794–800 Finchley Road,
London NW11 7UT
020 8455 1234
extensive showroom with
diverse lighting stock

WINDOWS

Artisan
01772 20355
catalogue of curtain
poles and finials

Eclectics
0870 010 2211 for mail
order
www.eclectics.co.uk
extensive collection of
main types of blinds

Prêt à Vivre
0845 130 5161
www.pretavivre.com
curtains or blinds by mail
order

Velux
www.velux.com
windows, skylights,
blinds
FABRICS AND LINEN

Between the Sheets
01249 821517
bed linen

**Chelsea Harbour
Design Centre**
London SW10
www.chelsea-
harbour.co.uk
large number of high-
quality/luxury furnishing
fabric companies are
based here

Malabar
31–33 South Bank
Business Centre, Ponton
Road, London SW8 5XP
020 7501 4200
Indian furnishing fabrics

**The Natural Fabric
Company**
127 High Street,
Hungerford, Berks
RG17 0DL
01488 684002
Indian cotton and silk,
Irish linen

Peacock Blue
0870 333 1555 for mail
order
linen and bedding

Pongees
28–30 Hoxton Square,
London N1 6NN
020 7739 9130
extensive range of silks

Warris Vianni
85 Golborne Road,
London W10 5NL
020 8964 0069
www.warrisvianni.com
huge collection of
fabrics from Europe and
Asia

Whaleys
Harris Court, Great
Horton, Bradford
BD7 4EQ
01274 576718
vast range of traditional
fabrics

The White Company
0870 160 1610
bed linen, table linen,
towels, nightwear, in
white only

ACCESSORIES

Alice & Astrid
020 8960 7790 for mail
order
www.aliceandastrid.com
home accessories from
India, mainly textiles

Antique Restorations
01959 563863 for mail
order
handles and fittings
Aria
295–296 Upper Street,
London N1 2TU
020 7704 6222
www.aria-shop.co.uk
accessories and
ornaments for the home,
some with designer
labels

Aspirations
190 Balls Pond Road,
London N1 4AA
020 7226 8575
ceramics, furniture,
sculpture, accessories
with exotic origins

David Wainwright
63/251 Portobello Road,
London W11 3DB
020 7727 0707
furniture, accessories
and ornaments from Asia

**Design Museum
Shop**
28 Shad Thames,
London SE1 2YD
020 7403 6933
www.designmuseum.org
accessories from all the
big names in design

Egg
36 Kinnerton Street,
London SW1X 8ES
020 7589 5070
fine glass and pottery
with a natural theme

Forgeries
01962 842822 for mail
order
handles and fittings

**Oxo Tower &
Gabriel's Wharf**
Oxo Tower Wharf,
Bargehouse Street,
London SE1
020 7401 2255
www.oxotower.co.uk
studios/shops of the
many artists and
craftspeople in
residence, producing
anything from china to
rugs to chandeliers

Plümo
0870 241 3590 for mail
order
www.plumo.com
handcrafted ornaments
and accessories (plus
clothes) by new
designers

Price's
110 York Road,
London SW11 3RD
020 7801 2030
large range of candles
for the home

FIREPLACES AND
STOVES

Acquisitions
24–26 Holmes Road,
London NW5 3AB
020 7482 2949
www.acquisitions.co.uk
fireplaces, surrounds,
tiles from period designs

**Anglia Fireplaces
& Design**
Anglia House, Kendal
Court, 1 Cambridge
Road, Impington,
Cambs CB4 4NU
01223 234713
www.fireplaces.co.uk
period-style and modern
solid fuel/gas fires

British Gas
0845 609 9595
www.gas.co.uk
mail order: gas and
electric fires and
surrounds

**Diligence
International**
Highbank House,
Up Somborne,
Stockbridge, Hants
SO20 6QZ
01794 388812
modern fires and
accessories from France

Flamewave Fires
The Farmyard,
Pearsons Green,
Brenthley, Tunbridge,
Kent TN12 7DE
01892 724458
www.flamewavefires
.co.uk
solid fuel stoves, and
convector boxes

The Hot Spot
53–55 High Street,
Uttoxeter, Staffs
ST14 7JQ
01889 565411
www.thehotspot.co.uk
extensive range of
stoves

Jetmaster Fires
Manor House Avenue,
Millbrook, Southampton,
Hants SO15 0AW
023 8077 4000
fires burning wood,
coal, gas

Modus Design
Studio House,
Miles Pit Hill,
London NW7 2RZ
01923 210442
modern solid fuel and
gas fireplaces

Ouzledale Foundry
PO Box 4, Long Ing,
Barnoldswick,
Colne, Lancs
BB8 6BN
01282 813235
www.ouzledale.co.uk
wood and solid fuel
stoves, Victorian-type
fireplaces

ARCHITECTURAL
SALVAGE

Andy Thornton
Architectural Antiques
Victoria Mills, Stainland
Road, Greetland,
Halifax, West Yorks
HX4 8AD
01422 377314
www.ataa.co.uk
huge selection of period
items

**Architectural
Heritage**
Taddington Manor,
Taddington,
Cutsdean, Cheltenham,
Gloucs GL54 5RY
01386 584414
www.architectural-
heritage.co.uk
salvaged stone and
marble fireplaces, oak
panelling

The House Hospital
9 Ferrier Street,
London SW18 1SW
020 8870 8202
reclaimed elements from
Victorian houses:
fireplaces, bathrooms,
radiators, doors etc

In Situ Antiques
Talbot Mill, Ellesmere
Road, Hulme,
Manchester M15 4JY
0161 839 5525
extensive range of
architectural salvage
materials

LASSCO
(London Architectural
Salvage & Supply
Company)
St Michael's Church,
Mark Street, Off Paul
Street, London EC2 4ER
020 7749 9944
www.lassco.co.uk
salvaged fireplaces,
flooring,kitchen/bathroom
fittings, radiators and
other elements

Original Doors
923 Endwell Road,
London SE4 2NF
020 7252 8109
restored old doors and
door furniture

Tower Reclaim
Tower Farm, Norwich
Road, Mendlesham,
Suffolk IP14 5NE
01449 766095
reclaimed bathrooms,
flooring, doors

**Victorian Wood
Works**
54 River Road,
Creek Mouth,
Barking, Essex
020 8534 1000
www.victorianwoodworks
.co.uk
vast range of reclaimed
flooring

Walcot Reclamation
108 Walcot Street,
Bath BA1 5BG
01225 444404
www.walcot.com
good selection of
salvaged elements:
furniture, fittings,
fireplaces, bathrooms,
flooring

Water Monopoly
16–18 Lonsdale Road,
London NW6 6RD
020 7624 2636
salvaged baths